SUPPLY
TEACHING

KS1

P1 to 3

AUTHORS
Ann Malpass and
Dorothy Tipton

EDITOR
Christine Harvey

ASSISTANT EDITOR
Dulcie Booth

SERIES DESIGNER
Anna Oliwa

DESIGNERS
Nari Sandhu
Anna Oliwa

ILLUSTRATIONS
Caroline Ewen

COVER ARTWORK
Andy Parker

**Text © 2002 Ann Malpass
and Dorothy Tipton
© 2002 Scholastic Ltd**

Designed using Adobe PageMaker
Published by Scholastic Ltd, Villiers House, Clarendon
Avenue, Leamington Spa, Warwickshire CV32 5PR
Printed by Bell & Bain Ltd, Glasgow

1 2 3 4 5 6 7 8 9 0   2 3 4 5 6 7 8 9 0 1

British Library Cataloguing-in-Publication Data
A catalogue record for this book is available from the
British Library.

ISBN 0-439-01976-1

ACKNOWLEDGEMENTS
Curtis Brown Ltd, London
for the use of an extract from *The
Wind in the Willows* by Kenneth
Grahame © 1907, The University
Chest, Oxford. Reproduced by
permission of Curtis Brown.

Every effort has been made to
trace copyright holders and the
publishers apologise for any
inadvertent omissions.

Contents

Ready to Go: Supply Teaching is intended to be an invaluable resource, offering practical suggestions for teachers who have been called into school at short notice. However, the ideas included can be adapted and modified by all teachers, not just supply teachers, to provide activities for a wide range of cross-curricular themes. The book has been divided into three useful sections for easy reference: Instant ideas, themes for two-day cover and themes for five-day cover.

The 'instant ideas' could be used on many occasions and are a good way to get to know the children quickly. They could also be useful resources for any teacher who is given unplanned and unexpected time with children, when there is not enough time to continue project work.

The second section contains activities for two-day cover on the themes of: Journeys, Wood, Colour, Communication, Homes and Underground. These are aimed at the supply teacher who has been asked to cover a class in an emergency, where specific programmes of study are not available in time for preparation to be made. The themes are broad based. Each activity within a theme is complete in itself, but has links with all the work undertaken in the two days. The activities cover English and mathematics as a main thrust and all other areas of the curriculum are included.

The third section provides activities for five-day cover on the themes of: Markets, The Wonderful Wizard of Oz, Messages and White. The activities cover the core subjects of English, mathematics and science, and the foundation subjects of history and geography. All are based on National Curriculum requirements. The themes in this section will either introduce the children to new but appropriate key ideas or reinforce concepts explored by the class teacher but using a different approach.

The themes can be adapted for a shorter time or extended for a longer period by the 'Now or later' section which appears at the end of each theme and each idea can be simplified or made more challenging as required. The photocopiable pages are useful resources to enhance and extend the suggested programmes of study.

PREPARE YOURSELF

This book will give you the opportunity to make appropriate preparations and be ready to go when you receive an unexpected telephone call. It is most important to have prepared a basic kit of items that you are sure to need, but also make use of the school's resources, including the photocopier, to ensure that you have plenty of material ready for the children. A suggested basic kit is:
- a good story book and/or anthology of poems
- a modern edition of the Bible and *Religions of the World* by Elizabeth Breuilly and Martin Palmer (Collins)
- digit cards, dominoes, alphabet cards, dice

- a collection of pictures and photographs
- a music tape suitable for listening, dance or discussion
- a whistle, trainers, track suit
- red, black and blue biros, thick black felt-tipped pen
- good eraser, ruler, sharp pencils, pencil sharpener
- Blu-Tack, glue stick, adhesive tape
- scissors
- self-adhesive stickers
- plain A4 paper
- own flip chart or board (for use in preparation)
- your reference number.

Other useful things to take:
- calendar pictures, Christmas and birthday cards
- old photographs and postcards
- suitable magazine pictures
- interesting objects
- collage materials
- dressing-up clothes
- natural materials (fir cones, conkers)
- travel brochures
- found materials (long tubes, egg boxes)
- simple games, particularly those suggested in the text.

What to do when the phone rings
- Take the name and telephone number of the school. Ask for directions.
- Ask for a contact name.
- Establish the age range of the children, brief details of the day's planning and the daily routine.
- Pick up your basic kit.

On arrival
- Find the contact teacher, who should provide you with a daily timetable.
- Take note of fire regulations and security arrangements.
- Enquire about the school's policy on behaviour and discipline and then try to be consistent with what usually happens.
- Establish yourself in the classroom and quickly acquaint yourself with its resources.
- Make yourself ready for the children with a prepared introductory activity.
- Register the children as quickly as possible and move on to the first main activity.
- Establish your routine for the day with the children.
- Adapt the programmes of study in this book to the school's timetable.

THE CHILDREN'S WORK

Each school will have a marking policy and this should be adhered to. Your contact teacher should give you this information. The children's work must be valued at all times and they will of course appreciate positive comments about their work. If the school's policy will allow, it can be rewarding for the children to present their work in individual project books and since most of the photocopiable pages included in this book are of A4 size these could all be clipped together.

Some children may try to take advantage of your position as a supply teacher, so in the longer term assess the standard of their work by looking at previous examples.

RECORDS

It is important that a record of the day's planning is available for the class teacher to see on return. Your assessment of the activities and of significant individual children will be appreciated. Usually there are planning sheets appropriate to each school for you to complete. Informal notes will also be welcome.

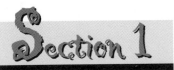
The ideas in this section are for:
■ consolidating previous work
■ introducing new concepts
■ encouraging quicker responses.

18 INSTANT IDEAS

RESOURCES

You will need photocopiable pages 6, 7 and 8. These can be made more durable for long-term use if copied onto a card and laminated, or if each idea is cut individually and placed in a box, folder, plastic wallet or ring binder. Keep these close at hand for immediate use. You should have a flip chart and a thick, brightly coloured pen, and the children will need a pen or pencil and paper. You will also need a collection of objects that vary in size and shape, a clock, a box of coins, a collection of pictures, a set of 'occupation cards' and a basket.

WHAT TO DO

The ideas are self-explanatory. Many of them are not new, but they are tried and tested. There are word games, number activities, wordstrings, memory games, limericks, spelling activities, drama suggestions and so on.

They can be used with a small group or with individual children, either to re-emphasise a point or when a child has finished a piece of work quickly. When using them with the whole class you might find it helpful to transfer the ideas to a flip chart. The key information words should be copied onto the chart and the children given a time limit in which to work the activity. There are many suggestions given for answers, but the list is not definitive and the children will doubtless find many more. Make sure that when an 'instant idea' is used there is time for the answers to be heard.

NOW OR LATER

■ Give the children three numbers, for example 1, 3 and 4. How many different ways can they arrange them to give 2 digit numbers? (13, 31, 43)
■ Create an 'Alphabet poem': *A is for animals that live in the zoo, B is for bears – let's watch what they do, C is for…* and so on.
■ Have two boxes, one labelled 'Nouns' the other 'Adjectives'. Jumble a number of cards with appropriate words on them and ask the children to sort and place them into the correct box.
■ Using the 'Nouns' and 'Adjectives' boxes, ask volunteers to take a card from either box, act out the word and the others respond.
■ Ask the children how many different ways they can make 10. (0 + 10, 8 + 2, 7 + 3, and so on.)

Word game – Farms

A Complete the word. Choose a letter.
B
C   FA_M   AN_M_L
D   TR_CT_R
E   _IG   C_IC_ _N
F   D_ _K   H_ _SE
G
H   M_C_   SP_ _AD_R
I   C_ _B_ _E   _I_K
J

K L M N O P Q R S T U V W X Y Z

Dominoes

Add or subtract.

How many? **(7 or 3)**

 × OR ÷

How many? **(15 or 6)**

Act it out

Driver	Postman	Dairy maid	Shopkeeper	Farmer	Teacher	Doctor	Nurse	Gardener	Secretary

- Make occupation cards.
- Ask a child to choose one.
- The child then mimes the job.
- Can anyone guess what it is?

How many words from… ?

Adventure

advent	vent	ten	ran	date
tar	enter	van	tan	eat
tear	tree	vane	rude	near
are	read	red	tread	dent
venture	reed	dan	ate	rate

Clocks

What time is it...

2 hours after?

1 hour after?

5 hours after?

3 hours before?

4 hours after?

2 hours before?

Hold up the clock.

Limericks

There once was a boy called Sam

Who ran as fast as you can

He fell on his nose

It was red as a rose

And looked like a piece of raw ham.

Write your own.

Acrostic animals

Will
Oliver
Ring
Mother?

Do
Onions
Grow?

Mother
Only
Uses
Stamped
Eggs

Brenda's
In a
Red
Dress

Can
Animals
Think?

Make your own.

Look at me

What do you see?

Describe an object.
What is it?

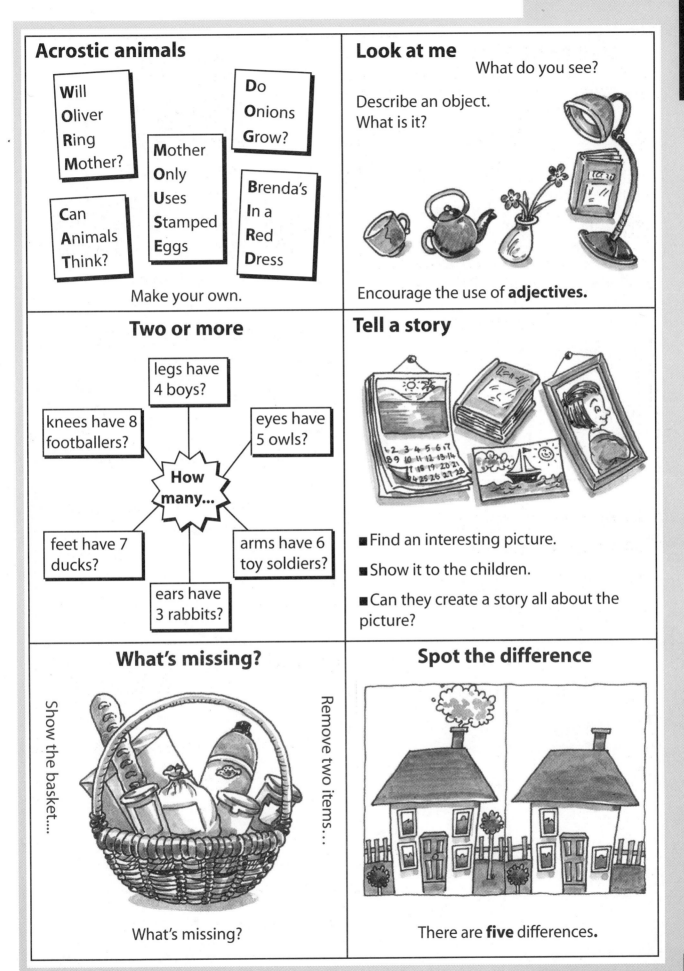

Encourage the use of **adjectives.**

Two or more

legs have
4 boys?

eyes have
5 owls?

knees have 8
footballers?

**How
many...**

feet have 7
ducks?

arms have 6
toy soldiers?

ears have
3 rabbits?

Tell a story

■ Find an interesting picture.

■ Show it to the children.

■ Can they create a story all about the picture?

What's missing?

Show the basket....

Remove two items...

What's missing?

Spot the difference

There are **five** differences**.**

Singing rhymes...
can you create more?

1 potato **2** potatoes **3** potatoes **4**
5 potatoes **6** potatoes **7** potatoes, more.

1 2 3 4 5, once I caught a fish alive
6 7 8 9 10, then I let it go again.

5 fat sausages sizzling in a pan
1 went bang and then there were **4**.

Cows and horses walk on **4** legs
Little children walk on **2** legs
Fishes swim in water clear
Birds fly up into the air. **1 2 3 4 5**.

How much?
Use boxes of coins.

My pencil costs **5p**

Show me the money.

My scissors cost **15p**

Show me the money.

My book costs **20p**

Show me the money.

My crayons costs **25p**

Show me the money.

Describe a...

colour
food
game
film
book
picture

dance
instrument
toy
person
animal
pet

Dictionary
Find words with…

6 letters beginning with **b** (bobble, border, borrow).

5 letters beginning with **h** (house, hello, heard).

4 letters beginning with **p** (push, pull, pink).

Wordstrings
How far can you go?

SUN → NICE → EXCITING → GOOD → DAY
HEAT ← MONTH ← WARM ← YELLOW ←
HEAT → TEA → AFTERNOON → NEW → WATER → RIPPLE

Jumbles

SPADE
BUILDING
DIGGER
CEMENT
SHOVEL
BRICKS
WATER
SAND
TILES
CONCRETE

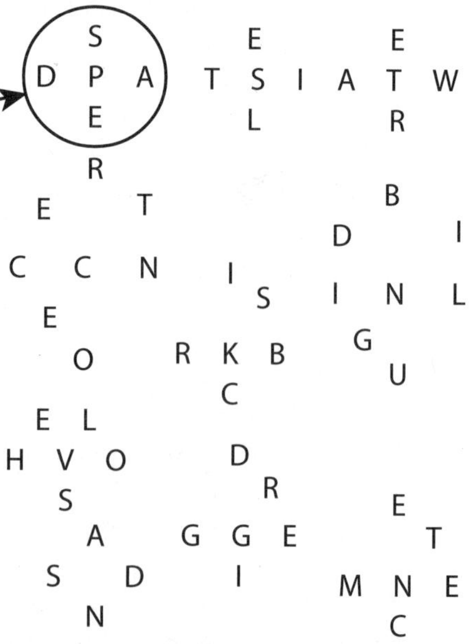

Ready to go! SUPPLY TEACHING

This section provides a wide variety of cross-curricular activities for two-day cover on the themes of Journeys, Wood, Colour, Communication, Homes and Underground.

JOURNEYS

RESOURCES

You will need:
- copies of photocopiable page 29 for each child, paper, writing materials (English)
- copies of photocopiable page 30 for each child, 12 chairs, Multilink, lollipop sticks or straws, number strips marked 1–20, digit cards (mathematics)
- an Ordnance Survey map, a play mat, blocks, toy railway track, blue material, Lego, toy farm animals, sand tray, paper and pencils (geography)
- a stone or other special object, a musical tape and a tape player (PSHE)
- a variety of collage materials relevant to the 'journey' theme, such as pictures of foreign countries, bus timetables or postcards, pre-cut thin card, marker pens, glue (art)
- mats and hoops (PE).

WHAT TO DO

English

Give each child a copy of Robert Louis Stevenson's poem 'From a Railway Carriage' on photocopiable page 29 and read aloud to them. Look more closely at the first four lines to show the children which words create the rhythm of the train moving along the tracks. What sort of train do the children think he is writing about?

Explain to the children what a simile is and draw their attention to the three in the poem – *fairies*, *witches* and *troops in a battle*. What other things do they think the poet might have used? Give a few examples, such as *rockets*, *planes*, *a lion* or *a racing car*. Ask them to list words that represent speed, such as *quicker*, *slower*, *crawling*, *zooming*. Then invite the children to combine the two lists and create their own similes, for example *quicker than my dog*, *slower than a snail*.

Read the poem again. Ask the class to imagine all the characters they might meet on this train, for example an engine driver, excited children, businesspeople, refreshment sellers. Talk about each character and encourage the children to describe what that person might be doing. If there are children who have never been on a train they might relate to the *Thomas the Tank Engine* stories by Rev W Awdry.

Ask each child to find a space for role-play and create situations for them to mime. For example tell them to imagine that they are passengers on a platform with a luggage trolley. What would they do if the luggage fell off? Develop this idea by asking the children to work in pairs creating interactive situations for them, such as a passenger asking the guard the way, two people chatting on the train and so on. Then invite some pairs to perform at the front of the class and get others to guess what they are doing.

OBJECTIVES

- experiencing rhythm in poetry; identifying similes and being involved in characterisation through mime **(English)**
- practising calculating and distinguishing between odd and even numbers **(mathematics)**
- visualising and creating a map **(geography)**
- recognising key religious places around the world **(RE)**
- taking personal responsibility for behaviour **(PSHE)**
- using a range of materials to create a picture **(art)**
- practising different body positions **(PE)**

Mathematics

Read aloud 'The dinosaurs' journey' to the children.

THE DINOSAURS' JOURNEY

10 dinosaurs went on a journey
They walked, and took their time
1 fell asleep, in a great big heap
And then there were only 9.

9 dinosaurs went on a journey
They flew so as not to be late
1 scratched his wing, the poor wee thing
And then there were only 8.

8 dinosaurs went on a journey
They decided to go to Devon
1 stubbed his toe and could not go
And then there were only 7.

7 dinosaurs went on a journey
They crawled amongst the sticks
1 lost his way, and decided to play
And then there were only 6.

6 dinosaurs went on a journey
They swam and splashed and dived
But one got drowned. He was never found
And then there were only 5.

5 dinosaurs went on a journey
They ran to a distant shore
1 cut his knee, oh deary me
And then there were only 4.

4 dinosaurs went on a journey
They paddled along on a tree
1 fell with a splash, and never got back
And then there were only 3.

3 dinosaurs went on a journey
They couldn't think what to do
1 wandered away, not seen to this day
And then there were only 2.

2 dinosaurs went on a journey
They wanted to find the sun
1 sat out all day and shrivelled away
And then there was only 1.

1 dinosaur went on a journey
He liked what he could see
He ran, he jumped, he leapt for joy,
He ran, he jumped, he leapt for joy,
Shouting, 'I'm glad there's only me!'

As you read ask them to anticipate the number which comes at the end of each verse. Ask if they know any more rhymes like this where numbers are added on, for example *1, 2, 3, 4, 5, once I caught a fish alive.* Practise counting on with the children from a given number in 1s, 2s and 3s.

Move on to give the children practical experience in adding on larger numbers from a given number. Give each child a copy of photocopiable page 30. Get them to fill in the numbers in the boxes and then draw their own journeys to practise adding on numbers.

Talk about odd and even numbers to establish the children's understanding of the concept. Then place six pairs of chairs together to represent a bus. Invite 12 children to enter the bus and make the point that you have an even number of people. Repeat this activity several times with different numbers of children to illustrate the difference between odd and even.

Give each child a random number of Multilink, straws or lollipop sticks. Ask them to put their objects into pairs. Explain that if they have an object left over, then they had an odd number of objects to start with. Talk with the children about their results. Have they made an odd number or an even number? Can they say why it is odd or even?

To reinforce the concept give each child a number strip marked 1–20 and ask them to colour the odd or even numbers, or you could play the game 'Odds and Evens'. Hold up digit cards to the class. Ask the children to shout out if they see that you are holding up two odd or two even numbers. Tell them to remain silent if you are holding up one of each.

Geography

Ask the children to imagine that you are all going on a journey. You might be going on holiday, to visit a relation or on a school visit. What will you see? Make sure they cover a variety of landscapes, such as roads, railways, rivers, towns, valleys, agricultural and arable land. Ask the children to think about a real journey they have been on and to describe some of the things they saw.

Show the children an Ordnance Survey map and show them what symbols are used to indicate special things and places. Allow the children to create maps of their own in one of the following ways:

■ As a class build a 3-D map on a play mat, using blocks for mountains, toy tracks for railway lines, pieces of blue material for rivers, Lego to make houses, farm animals for agriculture and so on.

■ Get the children to use the sand tray to create a 3-D map. Include some of the ideas suggested above.

■ Ask the children to draw pictures to create a pictorial map.

RE

Do the children know that a religious journey is called a pilgrimage? Have they any idea what that might mean? Discuss how religious people often want to visit an important place associated with their religion. Have any of the children, their parents or grandparents ever been on a pilgrimage? Talk about places that people of different faiths make pilgrimages to:

Many Christians visit Bethlehem (Jesus' birthplace), Nazareth (where Jesus spent his childhood) or Jerusalem (the place of Jesus' death and resurrection). Many Roman Catholic Christians go to Rome as it is the home of the Pope, the religious leader of the Roman Catholic Church.

Many Jews visit Israel, especially to say prayers at the remains of the Western Wall in Jerusalem.

Muslims try at least once in their lives to make a pilgrimage to Makkah, in Saudi Arabia, which they believe to be the site of the first House of God and the birthplace of the Prophet Muhammad.

There are Hindu pilgrimage sites all over India. Among the most important are sites on the River Ganges, especially the place where it flows through the city of Varanasi.

Every Buddhist country has its own places of pilgrimage, but the ones in the north of India associated with the life of Siddhartha Gautama, Buddha, are the most important.

Talk with the children about the kinds of things one might do on a journey such as these. Explain that there might be a lot of fun, music, dance and laughter. Ask if they would like to go on a pilgrimage one day and if so, where to? Encourage an open discussion about the different religions represented by the children in the class.

PSHE

Ask the children to sit in a circle. Discuss what they think is meant by the word *rules*. Why do they think they need rules on a journey? Talk about safety, thought for others and so on. Play some happy music and pass around a stone or a special object. Whoever is holding the object when the music stops should give a personal example of acceptable behaviour whilst on a journey.

Can they suggest rules that are used in the classroom, at home, in the playground, in their community? Prompt them towards ideas such as *I do as I am told, I behave properly, I keep the rules*.

To conclude, divide the children into small groups. Ask each group to imagine they are in either a railway carriage, a school bus, a car or a boat. Give them a short time to prepare a mime of a situation where they are being naughty on their journey and to then show how they feel they should behave. Which rules did they observe?

Art

Create a classroom train. Provide the children with sheets of thin card that have already been cut to a suitable size. Divide the children into groups and choose a child from each group to draw an outline on the card of either an engine, a passenger coach, a goods wagon or a mail coach. To achieve uniformity between the groups tell the children to make their coach as large as the card will allow. Give each group some collage materials and tell them to make a collage on their carriage. Then cut out the shapes for the children and help them to assemble the train as a wall display.

PE

Allow the children about ten minutes to warm up by asking them to walk and run forwards and backwards, to the left and to the right and to perform side steps.

Divide the children into pairs and ask each pair to share a mat. Tell the children that they should both remain on the mat whilst performing the following movements. Ask the children to lie straight out on the mat and then curl up into a ball. Then show them how to curl up and roll, sideways, forwards, backwards and from side to side.

Move the children away from the mats and ask them to change from curling to stretching. Tell them to work with their partner, copying each other as they curl and stretch. They could be standing or on the floor. Remind them to stretch every part of their bodies, including their fingers and toes. They should reach up as high as they can and then tuck themselves in as tightly as they can when they curl. Develop this by asking them to try doing the opposite to their partner's movements. How easy is it to do this? Explain that some creatures move in this way when journeying from one place to another, for example caterpillars, worms, snakes and centipedes. Ask some of the children if they would like to demonstrate being one of these creatures.

Finally, divide the children into groups of six and allocate three hoops to each group. Get three children to hold hoops a short distance apart while the other three curl and stretch, caterpillar-like, through the hoops. Then tell them to change over. Invite the children to look at other groups and lead them in making positive comments about each other's movements, such as *a tight curl, an imaginative stretch, a smooth movement.*

NOW OR LATER
■ Give the children a picture of a holiday destination. Ask them how they would travel there. Allow them to use their imagination to include air, sea, road and rail transport. (geography)
■ Warm the children up and then ask them to move around the room using their hands and feet, then travelling on their backs and tummies and then on their knees and elbows. Let the children watch each other and try to improve their movements. (PE)
■ Ask the children how they travel to school and talk to them about the different ways this information could be recorded. Get the children to record the information in the way they think is best. (mathematics)
■ Listen to a movement from Holst's *Planets Suite*. Talk about the images suggested by the music and then allow the children to paint their own interpretations of a journey to that planet. (music/art)
■ Get the children to make a model of a vehicle to travel in from construction materials. (D&T)

WOOD

RESOURCES
You will need:
■ a wooden box, flip chart or board, paper, writing materials (English)
■ wooden blocks, lollipop sticks, paper, writing materials (mathematics)
■ a range of musical instruments, tape recorder, flip chart or board (music)
■ a piece of wood (driftwood, bark, branch or a root), white cartridge paper or coloured sugar paper, charcoal, rubber (art)
■ a selection of percussion instruments such as tambour, small drum, woodblock, hard beater, tambourine, cymbal, triangle (PE).

WHAT TO DO
English
Take into the classroom an interesting wooden box and ask the children questions about it, such as: *Where might it have come from? Who do you think made it? Can you*

OBJECTIVES
■ recording imaginative ideas and stimulating the imagination **(English)**
■ understanding non-standard measures and using acquired knowledge to measure accurately **(maths)**
■ composing and performing in response to a poem **(music)**
■ creating an observational drawing **(art)**
■ using dance and movement to respond to music **(PE)**

13

describe what it is like? Write the adjectives the children use to describe the box on the flip chart, for example *small, cuboid, heavy*. Then ask the children to think about adjectives that relate specifically to the wood of the box and write these on the flip chart, for example *dark, patterned, shiny*.

Create an atmosphere of anticipation around the box. Ask the children what they think might be inside it. Start them off by suggesting objects such as a ring, a feather, a key, a message and so on. Ask them where they think the object might have come from, what it could be used for, who had it last and why it was put in the box. Develop the children's imagination in some of the following ways, according to their abilities:

■ Give an opening sentence, for example *I was so curious that I opened the box and…* Get them to write about what happened next.

■ Use a tape recorder to record the children's verbal observations on the opening of the box.

■ Ask the children to create a sequence of pictures to show what happened when the box was opened.

Mathematics

Tell the children that they are going to measure wooden things in the room using parts of their bodies. Explain that in the past craftsmen would have used a hand span to measure with, for example when measuring the distances between shelves in a bookcase. Show the children your hand span and demonstrate how to measure objects with it. Then ask the class to look at their own hand spans and encourage comments on the difference in sizes.

Can the children think of any other parts of their bodies that they could use to measure with? Show them how to use a digit, a forearm, a foot or a pace. Then ask the children to name wooden things around the room that could be measured in this way, such as a door frame or book box, and record these on the flip chart.

Divide the children into three groups and allocate something from the list for each group to measure. Allow the groups to choose the body part they think is the most suitable to measure their object with. When each group has measured its object, get them to change over. Then reassemble the class and compare the findings. Ask the children if the measurements were the same or different for each object and why they think they got the results they did.

Divide the class into groups again and invite them to come and measure the same wooden object, such as the width of the door. Give each group the same wooden block to measure with. Record the groups' results, which this time should be about the same. Discuss this with the children and highlight that a standard measure is important to achieve uniform measurements.

Split the class into pairs and distribute apparatus that could be used for measuring, such as lollipop sticks, pencils or wooden blocks. Tell the children that they should choose five wooden objects to measure and record their results. Children of a higher ability could use several tools to measure with and compare the different results they achieve.

Music

WHO IS THERE?

I walked into the forest green	(content, footsteps)
And looked around where I'd just been	(stop, anxious)
The trees were waving, their branches low	(curious, movement)
Leaves were swaying to and fro	(curious, movement)
My feet moved on in sluggish pace	(more anxious, slow)
I felt my heart begin to race	(worried, fast)
I wondered what I'd find in there	(fear, loud)
A dinosaur or a grizzly bear	(fear, very loud)
A voice called through the thick, dense wood	(still, vocal sound)
Telling me to run, I knew I should	(still, vocal sound)
But I was scared and cannot say	(fear, silence)
Why I turned and ran away.	(fear, fast)

Read the poem to the children and explain that they are going to describe it using music. Read the poem again, and ask the children what feelings come to mind after each line – fear, contentment, anxiety, hesitation. (Use the suggestions given in brackets in the text as a guide only.) Write the children's ideas on the flip chart and ask if they can decide what the sounds for each should be, for example fast or slow, loud or soft. Record the agreed sounds against the feelings on the flip chart. Then give each child an instrument, grouping them according to instrument family (wood, metal, skin, stringed). Get the children to compose a sound picture to describe the poem musically, pointing to the list on the flip chart to prompt the sounds. Tape the piece and play it back to the class, inviting constructive comments.

Art

Focus the children's attention on a piece of wood, such as driftwood, bark, a branch or a root. Ask them what they can see. (For example, knots, grain, holes.) Let them touch it and ask them how it feels. (For example, rough, lumpy, sharp.)

Ask how the children would draw the wood and what features they might like to reproduce. Give out the paper, charcoal and rubbers (see Resources). Put the wood in a visible place and ask them to draw their own interpretation of it, covering the paper with charcoal and using the rubber as a drawing instrument. Get the children to look at each other's work and encourage positive comments.

PE

Tell the children that you are going to make different sounds with percussion instruments and that they should respond to the sounds through movement. Play a slow beat on a tambour and tell the children to walk slowly around the hall, then speed up the beat and slow it down again, encouraging the children to respond to the change in rhythm. Shake a tambourine to make calm and frantic sounds and tell the children to act with smooth or frightened actions accordingly. They could respond with stopping and starting actions to the sound of a woodblock, or curling up and stretching out movements to the sound of a triangle and then an explosive cymbal crash.

Read again the 'Who is there?' poem and get the children to re-enact it all together with a leader or small group of children playing the instruments. Help the children to develop the movements suggested in the poem and then after a few practices perform the whole piece.

NOW OR LATER

■ Collect some pieces of bark for the children to experiment with bark rubbings. You will also need some wax crayons and paper for this. (art)
■ Find a short version of *Pinocchio* (Puffin children's classics). Read together with the class and enjoy. (English)
■ Divide the class in half and give each group either wooden instruments or metal instruments. Ask each group to make up a piece of music called Woody Woodman or Metal Man. (music)
■ Collect objects that have differing properties, such as stones, shells, string, and ask the children to record how each object's properties differ to those of a piece of wood (flexibility, hardness, softness and so on). (science)

COLOUR

OBJECTIVES

■ creating a greater awareness of the colours around us and using colour adjectives **(English)**
■ using the concepts of greater than and smaller than, and representing results in different ways **(mathematics)**
■ examining how light makes different colours **(science)**
■ exploring different emotions **(RE)**
■ using music to inspire design **(music/D&T/art)**

RESOURCES

You will need:
■ flip chart or board, paper, writing materials, card, coloured pencils, crayons or paint, a selection of toys, clothes and classroom objects in a variety of colours (English)
■ Multilink, counting sticks, three cardboard circles, flip chart or board, copies of photocopiable page 31 for each child, large-squared paper (mathematics)
■ bowl of water, pebble, mirror, tube, coloured paper shapes or beads, cardboard disc, sticky tape, pictures of rainbows (science)
■ a recording of 'Joseph's coat' (Rice and Webber), a selection of fabrics (brightly patterned and coloured), paper, pencils, coloured pencils or crayons (music, D&T, art).

WHAT TO DO

English

Read to the class the Christina Rossetti poem 'Colours' and discuss with them what colour words the poet uses.

COLOURS

What is pink? a rose is pink
By the fountain's brink.
What is red? a poppy's red
In its barley bed.
What is blue? the sky is blue
Where the clouds float thro'.
What is white? a swan is white
Sailing in the light.
What is yellow? pears are yellow
Rich and ripe and mellow.
What is green? the grass is green
With small flowers between.
What is violet? clouds are violet
In the summer twilight.
What is orange? why an orange
Just an orange!

Christina Rossetti

Talk with the children about the colours there are around us. Discuss the blue sky, the green grass, the yellow sun, the white daisy, the red traffic light, and then ask the children for more suggestions. Which do they think are the warmest colours and which the coldest colours? Ask them which are their favourite colours and why. Have some objects ready to show the children, such as toys, clothes, objects in the room and so on, and ask the children to use colour words as adjectives to describe them.

Re-read the 'Colours' poem. Ask the children if they think it includes all the colours of the rainbow in it? Can they name all the colours in a rainbow? Make a list of these on the flip chart. Ask the children to use the initials of each colour (ROYGBIV) to make an acrostic poem, such as *Red wellingtons, Orange sun, Yellow ducks, Green leaves*, and so on. Finally, get the children to draw and colour their own rainbow on which to present their acrostic poem and mount these on the wall.

Mathematics

Give each child a coloured counting stick, or coloured object or piece of Multilink. Ask the children to make a statement about it, such as *My object is long and thin and it is blue*. Explain that the objects are to be sorted into sets and ask how best they think this can be done. Guide them towards choosing two colour sets, for example blue and red. Have two large cardboard circles and label them *Blue* and *Red*, and ask each child to place their object in the correct circle. Ask them what they notice. What can be done with all the other colours? Give this group a name, for example 'Extras', and put this label onto another cardboard circle. Invite the children to place their remaining objects in it.

Discuss the results with them and talk about the ideas of 'greater than, less than, more than, fewer than'. Compile a simple tally chart of the results on the flip chart, asking the children to volunteer the amounts that should be entered under each heading. A visual representation of the results could be made by using Multilink or coloured blocks. Develop this idea as a whole-class activity by drawing a block graph using squared paper.

Give each child a copy of photocopiable page 31 and read through the information with the children. Explain that it shows a tally chart of the colour of a number of cars. Tell the children that they need to add up the total number of cars in each colour row.

Then tell the children that they are going to record the same information in a different way, using their tally charts to draw a block graph. Explain that to record the information on the squares provided they will need to label the horizontal row with the colour of each car and number the vertical squares starting with 1 at the bottom. Ask each child to transfer the information on their tally chart onto their block graph and to write some statements underneath it, such as *There are more blue cars than red cars*.

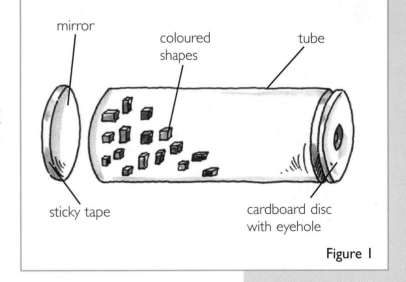

Figure 1

Science

Discuss rainbows with the children. Ask them when they last saw one. What do they think makes a rainbow? Tell the children that in 1666 Sir Isaac Newton discovered that when a beam of white light passed through a piece of glass (show one if possible) it splits into seven different colours. The colours are always the same and show in the same order – red, orange, yellow, green, blue, indigo, violet. Show the children some pictures of rainbows so that they can see this.

If the day is sunny, throw a pebble in a bowl of water and point out to the class the colours of the rainbow in the drops created by the splash. Alternatively, get the children to make a simple kaleidoscope (see Figure 1). Place the small coloured pieces of paper or beads inside a tube and attach a mirror at one end and a cardboard disc with an eyehole cut out of it at the other. Show the children how they can watch the moving coloured patterns.

RE

Introduce the children to 'Joseph and his coat of many colours' by reading the story to them.

JOSEPH AND HIS COAT OF MANY COLOURS

Joseph's father gave him a new coat. It was such a special coat because it was a brightly coloured coat and very different from anyone else's. His brothers were furious. They had never seen such a bright coat before and they were jealous. It

looked especially bright against the dirty, dusty roads. Joseph was happy but his brothers were mad. They went off on their own to talk about the coat, leaving Joseph behind.

'Go and find your brothers' said his father, so he did. When he found them they were still angry with him, so they took his coat and threw him down a hole. At first they were just trying to frighten him then they saw some travellers and they asked them if they would like to buy Joseph. The travellers agreed to take him with them. They sold him to the King to work for him.

Joseph grew bigger and stronger as the years passed by and one night the King had a dream. Joseph was quite good at telling people what their dreams meant and so the King sent for him.

'Your dream means that for seven years there will be plenty in this land,' said Joseph, 'and for seven years there will be nothing, there will be a famine.'

The King listened to him and asked what he should do. Joseph told him to store up the grain when there was plenty, ready to feed the people when there was nothing. This they did and the King made Joseph a very important man because he was so pleased with him.

The good years came and went and so did the famine. People in other lands were very hungry and they came to Joseph for food. Joseph's brothers were very hungry too and they went to the King to ask for a meal. They did not recognise their brother because he had grown up and was so important, but he recognised them. He was so pleased to see them again that he hugged them and told them who he was. He said that he would forgive them, then sent his youngest brother to fetch their father.

'Now I know why God sent me to Egypt,' said Joseph, 'it was to save my family.' And he was a very happy man.

Ask the children to describe how they think Joseph would have felt on receiving such a lovely coat. How do the children think he felt on being rejected by the brothers? How would *they* feel about getting a new coat, and about being rejected? Ask if they think they are possessive of their own things or if they are happy to share them.

Discuss with the children the moods Joseph must have experienced – joy, hurt, anger, loneliness, humility – and record these on the flip chart. Then tell the children they are going to 'mood act' the story. Divide the class into small groups and give one of the words on the list to each group. Get each group to create a short scene to show their mood, either acting out the Joseph story or a scene of their own choosing. Ask each group to perform to the whole class.

Music/D&T/Art
Play a recording of 'Joseph's coat' from Joseph and the Amazing Technicolour Dreamcoat (Webber and Rice, Novello Publications). There are many colours named in the last chorus. Ask the children how many they can hear. (There are 29.)

Discuss with the class what one needs for any coat (sleeves, length, collar, fastenings) and then show the children one. Ask them to design a coat for Joseph including all the things you have discussed. Tell them that it should be colourful. Try to have available a selection of brightly coloured patterned fabrics to show the children. Encourage them to design their coat in a pattern of their choice.

Now or later
■ Collect some really colourful autumn leaves or pressed flowers and show the children how to make rubbings of them. (art)
■ Try to create word links by asking the children to think of stories or rhymes that have a colour in their title, such as Red Riding Hood, Snow White, Blackbeard. (English)
■ Tell the children that every person's voice sounds different and that this is called the colour of the voice or the timbre. Get them to listen to the colour of each other's voices. Can they recognise voices when they cannot see the speaker? Blindfold a child and then point to a member of the class to be a speaker. (music)
■ Get the children to make some repeating colour patterns by drawing shapes and colouring them in. (mathematics)

COMMUNICATION

RESOURCES
You will need:
■ old and new postcards (old ones are easily obtained from second hand or antique stores), flip chart or board, card, paper, writing and colouring materials, magazine pictures relating to the postal service or travel (English)
■ boxes of coins and a selection of stamps (2p, 5p, 10p, 12p and 19p stamps), a purse with a 50p, 20p, 10p, two 5p, four 2p and two 1p coins in it (mathematics)
■ pictures of old (Victorian or Georgian) and modern postboxes (the post office have some excellent posters), copies of photocopiable page 32 for each child, paper, writing materials (history)
■ a selection of untuned instruments, such as drums, tambourines and woodblocks (music)
■ pictures of old and modern postboxes, paper, writing materials (D&T).

WHAT TO DO
English
Give out the old and new postcards for the children to handle and discuss with them what they notice about the differences, for example colours, the style of the pictures, stamps, handwriting.

Ask the children why we usually send a postcard. To whom might they like to send a postcard? Ask them to imagine that they are in their favourite place (you might

OBJECTIVES
■ composing a message and exploring the past and present tense (English)
■ using money in a practical way and experiencing changing money (mathematics)
■ understanding differences and similarities between past and present (history)
■ understanding what makes us happy and sad (PSHE)
■ communicating using rhythm (music)
■ creating a design (D&T)

need to discuss where this is with them) and are going to send a postcard to the teacher or to an imaginary friend.

Draw a postcard outline on the flip chart with an address on it and ask the children to copy this on to a piece of card, explaining that they are going to fill in the remainder of the postcard. First get them to make a draft, aiming to get three short sentences, a greeting and a name from most children, focusing their attention on capital letters and full stops. When they are happy with their sentences get the children to copy them on to their postcard. Then ask some of the children to share their greetings with the class. Finally, ask them to illustrate the other side of their card by drawing a picture or cutting out appropriate pictures from magazines. The postcards could be posted in a class postbox.

Using the flip chart, record the words in Figure 2 and ask the children to notice how each word has changed. Why would it need to change? Talk to them about the past and present tense of the words.

deliver	delivered
post	posted
receive	received
sort	sorted
arrive	arrived
walk	walked
change	changed
lift	lifted
code	coded
finish	finished
Figure 2 collect	collected

Then record the sentences in Figure 3 on the flip chart and ask the children to use the previous list of words to fill in the gaps.

> I _____ to the postbox to _____ a letter. It was _____ at the sorting office and the postman _____ it and _____ it to my grandma.
>
> Figure 3

The children can use some of the words to make sentences of their own, for example *I received a birthday card* or *I walked to the postbox*. Ask some of the children to read their sentences to the class.

Mathematics
Give each child a box of coins to look at and some stamps. Explain to the class that the coins will be used for buying stamps, and that sometimes they will be able to buy a stamp with one coin and sometimes they will need more than one.

Discuss coin values with the children holding up coins of different values. Then hold up different stamps, pointing out the cost of each in the corner. Ask the children which coins would be used to buy a 2p stamp, 5p stamp, 10p stamp, 12p stamp, 19p stamp. Can the children find the correct coins from their box? (There could be more than one answer.) Ask the children to select some stamps of different values and then place the appropriate coins they would need to buy them next to each.

Can they think of all the different combinations of coins they could use to buy each stamp? The children could also draw the stamp and coin combinations.

Have a look at the coins with the children again. Ask them how much change they will get from 50p if they buy a 2p stamp. A 5p stamp? A 10p stamp? A 12p stamp? A 19p stamp? Adjust the stamp values according to the abilities of the children. Finish by asking how much money they think they would have left if they bought all the stamps with a £1 coin?

Take the purse of coins into the classroom (see Resources) and show the money to the children and ask how much there is in total (there is £1). Invite suggestions of items that they might buy to write a letter with for less than £1 (pencil, pen, notepad, rubber and so on).

Tell the children that you are going to be a customer in their shop. You want to buy different items and you will need them to give you change. Present different scenarios, such as: *I am buying a postcard and it costs 10p, how much change will I need from 20p?* Give the money in your purse to a child and ask them to give you change. Then divide the class into pairs and give each pair the equivalent of £1 in change to play the same game. Some children may need to work with 20p or 50p before moving to £1.

History

Discuss with the children how the postcard would have been delivered in their great-grandparent's day. Talk about mailbags, hand-sorting, mail trains, deliveries by bicycle, horse, train and on foot. If possible have pictures of old postboxes for the children to see. Do the children know how the postal system has changed since then? Make sure that you mention postal address codes, standard sizes, mechanised sorting, conveyer belts and fork-lift trucks. Explain how Rowland Hill, in 1840, introduced the idea of buying a stamp at a post office to put on a letter, postcard or parcel, which could then be sent anywhere in the British Isles for a standard amount.

Ask the children to imagine that a postcard is to be sent from their town to the nearest seaside resort. Where do they think this would be? How would the card get there? Give the children a copy of photocopiable page 32, which shows pictures of different methods of mail delivery, now and in the past. Ask them to cut out the pictures and sequence them in two lines under the headings: *My great-grandparent's mail delivery* and *My mail delivery*. The children could then write some text under one of the sequences beginning, *I am a postcard and I have been on a journey. First I was…*

PSHE

Ask the children to talk about why we send postcards and letters. Who do they like to hear from and who likes to hear from them? Point out to them that sometimes these messages are happy and sometimes they are sad. Which type of message would they rather receive and why?

Divide the children into pairs and get one child to be the sender of a message and the other to be the receiver of the message. Ask them to mime sending and receiving a happy message and then a sad message. When they have practised a few times get them to perform their mimes for the rest of the class.

Music

Sit the children in a circle. Talk to them about how messages were sent in the past using voices and drums. Choose a leader (it does not have to be the teacher) and ask them to whisper a message to the person next to them. This is passed on as a whispered message around the circle until it returns to its starting point. Ask the leader if the message is the same. Change the leader and try again.

Get the leader to clap a short message to a neighbour who passes it on, continuing around the circle. Ask if this message has changed when it comes back to the leader. What do the children think of this way of sending information?

Then get the leader to clap a short rhythm as a message and point to someone else in the circle who must think of their own rhythm message and clap back. The leader should then clap a short message and point to someone else and so on. Let a few children in the circle try this and tell them how messages have been sent by using rhythms. Do the children know about Morse code or African drum messages?

Take two untuned instruments, such as a drum, a woodblock or a tambourine. Give one to a child and use the other yourself. Tap out a simple rhythm message and ask the child to reply with their own instrument. Try this with a few different children before dividing the class into pairs and asking them to send and receive messages between them with their own instruments. It will be noisy, but great fun! This can also be done by clapping or clicking messages. Choose a few children to perform their rhythm messages to the class.

D&T
Show the pictures of postboxes from different eras to the children. Ask them to volunteer what similarities and differences they can spot and how they have changed (round tops, pyramid tops, holes in the wall and so on). Focus on one of the postboxes and discuss with the class its shape, size and colour. What do the children think would be the most suitable materials to use to make a model of one of these (card, wood, glue, paint)?

Ask each child to choose a type of postbox they like most (for example, Georgian, Victorian or modern). Tell them they are going to draw a design to make their postbox. Once they have drawn it ask them to write a list underneath of suitable materials they could use to construct it. Then get them to draw a picture sequence to show the assembly order.

At some time the children should be encouraged to make their postbox (this could be at home) and then a display to show the postboxes through the ages could be set up.

NOW OR LATER
■ Sing a French song with the children, such as *Frère Jacques*, and discuss with them how people in different countries communicate with each other. (English)
■ Invite a speech therapist to show the children how to communicate through sign language (this information can be obtained from your local health authority). (English)
■ Get the class to make a poster that will communicate information about a forthcoming event, such as a book fair. (art)

HOMES

RESOURCES

You will need:
■ an OHT of photocopiable page 33, a selection of shoes, such as a wellington boot, slipper, sandal; paper, writing materials (English)
■ a selection of 2-D shapes, such as pattern blocks or plastic shapes, of squares, rectangles, triangles and so on; a variety of 3-D shapes, including cubes, cylinders, cuboids, cylinders and triangular prisms (these could be in the form of boxes and tins easily found in the home), flip chart or board (mathematics)
■ pictures of local homes and pictures of homes from other countries (both inside and outside of the homes) – mud huts, tepees, and so on (geography)
■ plastic pots, rubber bands, a selection of materials and fabrics, some that are waterproof and some that are not, such as cotton, wool, plastic, leather, paper or rooftile (science)
■ paper, paint and brushes, writing and drawing materials (RE)
■ pictures of beehives, flip chart or board, paper, writing and drawing materials, scissors, card, glue (enough for all the children) (art)
■ dowels, twigs, wood, lollipop sticks, straws, scissors, string, cotton, sticky tape, covering materials such as cotton, wool, plastic, leather or paper (D&T).

OBJECTIVES

■ developing ideas for characterisation and creating a simple rhyme **(English)**.
■ recognising the properties of 2-D and 3-D shapes and using knowledge of shape **(mathematics)**
■ recognising similarities and differences in homes **(geography)**
■ exploring the waterproof properties in materials **(science)**
■ discussing happy and sad feelings **(RE)**
■ creating an observational drawing or painting **(art)**
■ constructing a framework **(D&T)**

WHAT TO DO

English

Read to the children the nursery rhyme 'There was an old woman who lived in a shoe' from photocopiable page 33. Start by asking the children to think of words beginning with *sh–* and compile a list.

Then talk about the rhyme with the children. Show the children the selection of shoes, and invite each child to imagine a character that might live in one of them. Would any child like to tell the class about their imaginary character? Start to build together an oral picture of life in one of the shoes. Encourage imaginative descriptions, for example *My name is Tiny Centipede and I live in a green wellington boot that stands by the door of an old cottage.* Ask the children to draw a picture of this character and to write a description of it.

Read the nursery rhyme again to the class. Display photocopiable page 33 on an OHT, covering up some of the nouns, for example *shoe, children, woman*. Ask the children to predict which word is missing whilst reading the text aloud with them.

Using the OHT, ask the children to find the pairs of words which rhyme, for example *shoe/do, bread/bed*. Then, give the children a list of other nouns and encourage them to offer words that rhyme with these.

Finish by asking the children if they can create simple poems starting with each other's names, such as:

Ewan Grainger lived in a bog.
He went to Bognor and took his dog.

Ask the children to read their rhymes to the class.

Mathematics

Ask the children to draw a simple square house with a triangular roof and a rectangular chimney. Introduce the concept of 2-D shapes by talking about these three shapes. Ask the children if they can find any of these shapes in the classroom. Take them on a 'shape walk' or look through the window to see how many of the shapes can be seen in the homes in their area. Talk about the properties of each shape – how many corners and how many sides the shapes have, and how each shape differs from the others.

Divide the class into groups and give each group a selection of the 2-D shapes you have collected. Ask the children to sort these into sets of triangles, squares, large circles, small circles and so on. Circulate among the groups and discuss the activity with the children. Ask them to suggest other criteria for sorting, for example into three-sided and four-sided shapes instead.

On the flip chart draw a simple square house with a triangular roof and ask the children to copy it three times. Then get them to draw three different houses by drawing a variety of shapes onto each house template.

Take into the classroom the selection of 3-D shapes (see Resources). Look at them with the children and introduce the concept of 3-D shapes. Focus on the faces, edges and corners of the shapes.

Science

Show the children pictures of different homes and discuss how the homes are constructed and what materials are used to build them. Ask them to consider what happens when it rains. Do their homes keep out the rain?

Provide the children with the selection of waterproof and non-waterproof materials and fabrics. Ask the children to predict which will be waterproof. Why do they think this?

Split the children into groups and tell them they are going to test the materials. Talk to them about fair testing. How do they think they should test the materials? What are the variables? Prompt the children into suggesting that the materials should be different but each piece should be the same size and have the same amount of water poured on to it. Give each group some small plastic pots, a selection of the materials and rubber bands. Explain that when they have cut their material to size and labelled each piece, they can fix them one at a time over the top of the pot and pour the water on. Get them to record their results. Discuss these with the children and ask them which they would use to build a home. Which do they think would offer the best protection?

Geography

Show the children the pictures of the inside and outside of homes near where they live. Ask them what rooms they can see? Talk about what rooms there are in their own homes and what they do in each of them. Point out that all homes have somewhere to wash, cook, sleep, sit and relax. Also discuss with them how we all use lighting, water and heat in our homes.

Move towards focusing on homes in other parts of the world that do not have the same facilities. Can the children think of any places where the types of homes that people live in are different? Lead them towards talking about caves, tents, mud huts, houses on stilts, and show them the pictures of homes such as African huts or Bedouin tents. Ask the children to discuss these. How are they different from the types of homes in their locality? Can they see similarities? Do these homes have lighting, water and heat?

Take the children through a day living in one of these homes and ask them to think about how they would sleep, eat, wash and play in them. Ask the children to draw a picture of a home of their choice and to draw their ideas of how they think people would wash, eat and sleep in that home. Help the children to cut the pictures out and make into a class concertina book.

RE

Tell the children the parable of 'The lost coin'.

THE LOST COIN

Jesus told his disciples and the crowd of people that were following him a story about a woman who lost a coin.

The woman lived in a typical Israeli house with a flat roof and steps on the outside. There was a place to sit on the roof and very little furniture inside the house, and because of the heat and the sand it was very dusty. Jesus told that the woman had lost one of her ten silver coins.

'What did she do?' Jesus asked. 'Did she just sit around and forget it? No, she swept the corners and searched everywhere until she found it.'

Jesus went on to say that when she had found the lost coin she ran outside to share her good news with her neighbours. They might even have had a party because she was so happy to have found the lost coin. Jesus was trying to tell the disciples and those listening that that is how God feels, each time he finds someone who has been lost and has found him again.

Quiz the children about the story. What kind of house did the woman live in? Why was she able to sweep through the house easily until she had found the coin? Have the children ever lost anything special? How did they feel? Happy or sad? Ask the children what things make them sad. What things make them happy? They could write about this, or draw or paint a happy face and a sad face.

Art

Ask the children if they know what sort of home bees live in. Ask if any of them have seen a beehive. Have some pictures to show them in books or on the Internet, or alternatively you could draw one on the flip chart. Then ask them to draw or paint their own beehive.

D&T

Focusing on the structure of a tepee, talk about how Native Americans traditionally used these as their homes, because they were easy to build, transport and were warm. Provide a selection of dowels, twigs, wood, lollipop sticks and straws. Discuss which would be the easiest for them to use to make a framework for a model tepee, for example straws might be easier to cut than dowel or wood, which might need a saw. How many will they need? Suggest that at least three are required. How will they be joined? (Have string, cotton, sticky tape, and so on, at hand.)

Discuss with the class the type of materials that were traditionally used by the Native Americans and refer back to the science investigation (see page 24) relating to waterproof materials. Which material would the children choose to cover their model's framework? Will this keep the rain out? Ask the children to form pairs and then give them the materials of their choice to make their model tepee with.

Ask the children what they think it would be like to live in a tepee and how they think it would differ from their own homes.

NOW OR LATER

■ Talk about creatures that live in a tree. Give the children the opportunity to collage a large tree picture and include homes for animals such as woodpeckers, rabbits and squirrels. (science)

■ Choose rooms in the house and ask the children to show in role-play what things might be going on, such as cooking and eating in the kitchen, washing and cleaning their teeth in the bathroom. (English)

■ Listen to 'March Past of the Kitchen Utensils' by Vaughan Williams. Compose your own march using anything that can be found in the home, for example wooden spoons, baking tins, forks and so on. (music)

UNDERGROUND

OBJECTIVES

■ sequencing a story and understanding its structure; imagining a situation and writing about it using appropriate language **(English)**
■ estimating the difference between light and heavy objects and checking them using a balance **(mathematics)**
■ recognising that all animals need food and water to stay alive; developing knowledge of the concept of food chains **(science)**
■ relating descriptive music to movement **(music)**
■ using a range of textured materials **(art)**
■ experiencing different speed through movement **(PE)**

RESOURCES

You will need:

■ sentence cards (see box on page 27), flip chart or board, copies of photocopiable page 34 for each child, paper, writing materials (English)
■ stones, fossils, slate, coal, wooden blocks, pencil tin, balance scales, flip chart or board, root vegetables such as potatoes, carrots, parsnips and onions; a selection of objects to balance – Multilink, conkers, marbles (mathematics)
■ books or a CD-ROM to show what animals eat; card, string (science)
■ untuned instruments – tambourine, triangle, drum; tuned instruments – chime bars, xylophone, glockenspiel; wire brush, tape recorder, blank tape (music)
■ collage materials – straw, cellophane, fur fabric, corrugated paper, tissue paper, sand, card, access to word processors (art)
■ hoops, benches, climbing frames, skittles, mats and a whistle (PE).

WHAT TO DO

English

Read aloud to the class the extract from *The Wind in the Willows* by Kenneth Grahame.

The Mole had been working very hard all the morning, spring-cleaning his little home. First with brooms, then with dusters; then on ladders and steps and chairs, with a brush and a pail of whitewash; till he had dust in his throat and eyes, and splashes of whitewash all over his black fur, and an aching back and weary arms. Spring was moving in the air above and in the earth below and around him, penetrating even his dark and lowly little house with its spirit of divine discontent and longing.

It was small wonder, then, that he suddenly flung down his brush on the floor, said 'Bother!' and 'O blow!' and also 'Hang spring-cleaning!' and bolted out of the house without even waiting to put on his coat. Something up above was calling him imperiously, and he made for the steep little tunnel which answered in his case to the gravelled carriage-drive owned by animals whose residences are nearer to the sun and air. So he scraped and scratched and scrabbled and scrooged, and then he scrooged again and scrabbled and scratched and scraped, working busily with his little paws and muttering to himself, 'Up we go! Up we go!' till at last, pop! his snout came out into the sunlight, and he found himself rolling in the warm grass of a great meadow.

Discuss the passage with the class focusing on the mole. Ask the children: *What was the mole doing?* What do they think it would be like in his home under the ground?

Read again the last paragraph. Can the children remember the *scr–* words? Ask them to help make a list of these and write them on the flip chart. Can the children think of any more words to add to the list? Then give the word *dig*. Can the children think of other –ig words? Give a few examples, such as *pig*, *big* or *fig* and then write the children's list on the flip chart.

Some children could then move on to work with sentence cards, such as:

> The mole began to dig.
> He scratched at the soil and made a hole.
> The sun shone through.
> He squeezed through the hole.

Ask them to order these, copy and then illustrate them.

Older or more able children could write their own version of the story. Give them the opening sentences: *The mole made for the steep little tunnel which led to the fresh air above. He began to dig. He…* Invite the children to read some of their stories to the class.

Give the children a copy of photocopiable page 34 and ask them to form pairs. Invite them to imagine walking down the steps. What would it be like? Dark, gloomy, smelly, damp, slippery? How would they feel? Scared, cold, shocked? Write down their suggestions on the flip chart. Then ask the children to use some of the words to complete the poem.

Encourage them to extend the poem by adding their own verse. Share some of the children's verses with the class.

Mathematics

Talk to the children about some of the materials that can be found underground – fossils, slate, stones and coal. Try and have some of these for the children to handle. Focusing on a medium-sized object, such as a stone, ask them to find things in the classroom that they think weigh the same, for example a wooden block or a pencil tin. Then ask them to compare the weight of the objects. Are they lighter, heavier or the same? Make three areas with captions marked *lighter*, *heavier*, *the same as* and encourage the children to put other objects in the correct set. Extend the activity by using a balance to check the weight of each object. The children could then record the results on a chart.

Working in small groups, invite the children to look at the root vegetables. How are they grown? Where do the children think they would find them? (Underground.)

Ask the children to order the vegetables from the lightest to the heaviest and to write down this order. Then choose either Multilink, conkers or marbles to weigh each vegetable using the balance. The children should record their results in terms of how many Multilink or conkers are used and then order the vegetables from the lightest to the heaviest again. Is the order the same as before?

Science

Can the children think of other animals that live underground? Mention rabbits, rats, foxes and so on. Why do they think these animals live underground? Talk about warmth and protection. Ask them how they think these animals have adapted to living underground? Point them towards thinking about characteristics such as small eyes, claws and strong legs. What do they think animals need to live underground? Explain that they need the same as animals who don't live underground – food, water, air and heat.

Using the collection of books or a CD-ROM, allow the children to find out what different creatures eat. When they are ready, go on to look at the concept of the food chain. Establish with them that all food chains begin with green plants and give examples, such as *grass – rabbit – fox*; *soil – worms – badger*.

Allow the children to work in groups to make a food-chain mobile. They will need three card circles and some string. In the first circle, which will be at the bottom of the mobile, ask the children to draw green plants. In the other circles they should draw pictures of the creatures that eat the plants and so on up the food chain. When complete the circles should be joined together with string. (See Figure 4.)

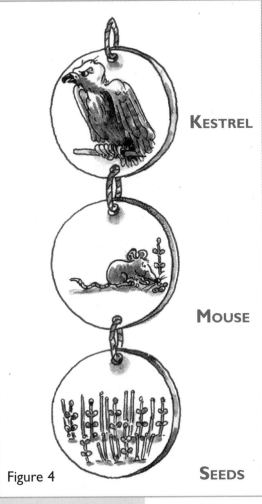

KESTREL

MOUSE

SEEDS

Figure 4

Music
Ask the children to make high and low sounds with the tuned instruments – chime bars, xylophone, glockenspiel – and fast and slow sounds using the untuned instruments – tambourine, triangle, drum. Can they find instruments that can play both fast and slow, and high and low?

Re-read the extract from *The Wind in the Willows* to the class. Ask them to suggest phrases which they could use to tell the story musically, such as *he scraped and scratched and scrabbled… till at last, pop!* (use a wire brush on a drum and then bang it) or *Spring was moving in the air above* (use triangles). Practise the order the sounds need to be played in to tell the story and then ask half the class to act it out whilst the other half plays the musical sequence. Make sure the children change over so that both groups are able to play and act. Tape the music if you wish.

Art
Ask the children to imagine that they are moles. Ask: *What would it be like living underground? Would it be dark? Would you see different rocks and soils? Would it be damp?*

Using a variety of the textured materials you have collected, allow the children to create an underground picture of their choice (individually or in pairs). Let the children use word processors to write a caption for their picture. Mount the pictures on the wall or assemble them in a book entitled *Underground*.

PE
Explain to the children that they are going to practise some of the movements that a mole might make.

Warm the children up and then read the following sentence from *The Wind in the Willows* extract: *Up we go! Up we go! till at last, pop! his snout came out into the sunlight.* Ask the children to make a high shape followed by a low shape. Can they vary the speed at which they make the shapes? Suggest that they work with a partner to make these shapes. Can they include movements that involve going under or over their partner? Encourage them to perform crouching, jumping, climbing and crawling sequences. Choose children to demonstrate good examples. Allow time for the children to practise and refine their sequences and then arrange different apparatus in the corners of the room (hoops, benches, skittles, mats). Tell the children that on a whistle signal they can move to a corner of their choice and work on the apparatus using the movements practised previously. Whilst changing corners they should perform 'bunny jumps'.

NOW OR LATER
■ Talk about tunnels and allow the children to generate their own design for a tunnel. Make sure they take into consideration criteria such as width, height, strength and shape. (D&T)

■ Look at pictures depicting scenes from a coal mine. Ask the children to describe what they can see and discuss the different jobs the miners are doing. Set up a drama activity in which the children can demonstrate actions of the different activities being performed by the miners. (history)

■ Show the children some fossils and talk about what the children think made the shapes. Use this as a stimulus and get the children to draw similar patterns. (art)

From a railway carriage

Faster than fairies, faster than witches,

Bridges and houses, hedges and ditches;

And charging along like troops in a battle,

All through the meadows the horses and cattle:

All of the sights of the hill and the plain

Fly as thick as driving rain;

And ever again, in the wink of an eye,

Painted stations whistle by.

Here is a child who clambers and scrambles,

All by himself and gathering brambles;

Here is a tramp who stands and gazes;

And there is a green for stringing the daisies!

Here is a cart run away in the road

Lumping along with man and load;

And here is a mill and there is a river:

Each a glimpse and gone for ever!

Robert Louis Stevenson

How many travellers?

Car park

11 cars parked

5 more cars came

11 + 5 = ☐

Train

16 children   17 children

☐ + ☐ = ☐

Boat

☐ + ☐ = ☐

Bicycle

All children cycled to school

15 were at school

22 were travelling

☐ + ☐ = ☐

Aeroplane

13 crew   57 passengers

☐ + ☐ = ☐

Walking

Sponsored walk

Walk in groups of 3

☐ + ☐ + ☐ + ☐ = ☐

Draw your own journeys

Space rocket

☐ + ☐ = ☐

School bus

☐ + ☐ = ☐

Colourful cars

Colour	These cars went past the window	Total numbers of cars
White		
Blue		
Green		
Red		

Use the tally chart to draw a block graph			
7			
5			
2			
1			
White	Blue	Green	Red

What do you notice?

Name   Date

How has it changed?

Cut out the pictures and sort them into two groups – one showing your great-grandparent's letter being sent and delivered, the other showing your letter. Can you put each group into the correct sequence?

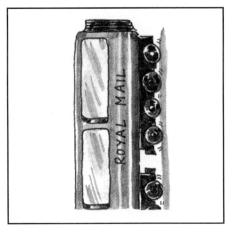

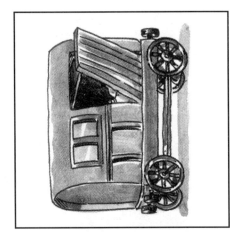

Name

Date

There was an old woman
who lived in a shoe

There was an old woman who lived in a shoe,

She had so many children she didn't know what to do;

She gave them some broth without any bread;

She whipped them all soundly and put them to bed.

Name _____   Date _____

Down in the cellar

Down the _____ steps.

Into the _____ cellar.

It was _____ and _____ , _____ and _____

My hands touched _____

and I was _____.

Now write your own verse.

Ready to go! SUPPLY TEACHING

This section provides a wide variety of cross-curricular activities for five-day cover on the themes of Markets, The Wonderful Wizard of Oz, Messages and White.

MARKETS

RESOURCES

You will need:
■ a shopping basket full of supermarket items such as apples, carrots, orange juice and so on, paper, writing materials, flip chart or board, copies of photocopiable page 57 for each child (English)
■ a selection of 1p, 2p, 5p and 10p coins, a purse, a selection of pick-and-mix sweets, a money box, boxes of coins with 1p, 2p, 5p and 10p coins in (enough boxes for one between each pair of children), flip chart or board, thin card, writing and colouring materials, scissors, copies of photocopiable page 58 for each pair (mathematics)
■ cress seeds, paper towels, dishes, observation chart (science)
■ paper, writing materials, flip chart or board (history)
■ a shopping basket filled with home-grown and foreign-grown foods such as potatoes, carrots, onions; melon, kiwi fruit, mango; flip chart or board, paper, writing materials (geography)
■ tape recorder, mood tapes (PSHE)
■ tape recorder, blank tape (music)
■ paper plates, small boxes, straws, papers, shells, pebbles, string, access to computers (art)
■ a selection of plastic shapes (circles, squares, triangles), paper, writing materials (D&T)
■ pictures of Covent Garden in London, mats (PE).

WHAT TO DO

English

Take into the classroom a shopping basket full of interesting items that are easily found in the supermarket, such as apples, carrots, orange juice and so on. Hold up some of the items and invite the children to describe them as accurately as possible using adjectives.

Choose six children to stand in front of the class and give the first child an item from the basket. Invite this child to make a statement about the item, such as: *I have a tin of beans.* Then ask a second child to add another statement, such as: *I have a tall tin of beans.* Child 3 should follow with a further statement, such as: *I have a tall tin of beans and they are orange.* Continue in this way until a child either runs out of ideas or cannot remember what has been said. Then ask the class to write their own long, descriptive sentences about an item from the basket. Finish by getting them to share their ideas.

OBJECTIVES

■ using adjectives effectively; using language persuasively; ordering lists alphabetically; using rhyming words and understanding characterisation **(English)**
■ recognising a range of coins and adding different coin values together to make a given amount **(mathematics)**
■ understanding what plants need to grow **(science)**
■ comparing past and present foods **(history)**
■ discovering where foods come from around the world **(geography)**
■ experiencing different moods **(RE/ PSHE)**
■ exploring the rhythm of words **(music)**
■ using collage materials **(art)**
■ using wheels and axles **(D&T)**
■ moving in a specific way **(PE)**

Take the children on an imaginary walk around the supermarket, getting them to picture some of the labels they might see around the goods, for example *3 for the price of 2, buy one get one free, sale, reduced.* Ask the children to write down some ideas for their own labels and to share them with the class. Choose some of the best ideas and tell the children they are going to include them on a class poster to advertise goods, explaining that this could be used to entice people to buy. Get the children to design a poster and write their labels on it.

Discuss with the children what their favourite foods are. Write them on a flip chart and then, as a class, put them into alphabetical order. Give each child a copy of photocopiable page 57 and tell them to write their own lists of favourite foods. Some children will be able to write their lists in alphabetical order.

Ask the children to give you rhyming words connected with food, for example *apple/dapple, plum/thumb, tin/bin.* Then read the rhyme 'We're going to the market' to the class and invite them to suggest the missing word at the end of each verse. Try reading it again to see if the children can find more rhyming words.

WE'RE GOING TO THE MARKET

We're going to the market
Why don't you come?
There's John and Jasmine
And Harminda's _____

Buying lots of goodies
Is always nice
Sausages, potatoes
Eggs and _____

We pay the stall holder
With our money
He sometimes gives the wrong change
And thinks it's _____

Carrying the bags home
Is always a lark
They rip, they tear
In the car _____

Home we go
We've had lots of fun
A cup of juice, a biscuit
And a game in the _____

Read to the class the rhyme 'To market, to market to buy a fat pig'. Re-read it inviting the children to join in by anticipating the final words – *jig* and *jog*. Give the children the first line of the rhyme again and add a different ending, for example *To market to market to buy a fat yoghurt* and ask them to join in with a new rhyming ending to the next line, such as *Home again, home again, let's take it to Robert*. Finish by asking the children to write a version of their own.

To market to market to buy a fat pig
Home again, home again jiggety jig

To market to market to buy a fat hog
Home again, home again jiggety jog.

Invite a class discussion about the people who work in a supermarket, such as sales assistants, shelf stackers, managers. Ask the children how much they know about these jobs. Encourage any children who know someone working in a supermarket to talk about the jobs. Then divide the class into small groups, giving each group a job, such as a customer or supervisor, to create a situation around this job and act it out. Ask each group to perform their scenario in front of the class.

Mathematics

These activities are more suitable for children of a lower ability. However, the activities can be easily adapted for any child's capabilities by simply changing the coinage.

Have a number of 2p coins hidden on your person. Show a coin to the children and ask if they recognise it. Show them another 2p coin and ask how much money they think they will have if the two coins are added together. Find more coins and each time show them to the children and ask them to keep adding up the total. Use 1p coins in the same way.

Label the sweets (see Resources) with clearly visible prices. Show the children different combinations of sweets and ask how they would pay for them using 1p and 2p coins.

Show the children a purse and find inside 1p, 2p and now 5p coins. Look at each of the coins with the children and show them how to recognise the differences. Talk to them about how to use the coins in different combinations. Then arrange groups of different coins together and get the children to tell you how much there is in total each time.

Show the children a money box and get them to speculate on how much money is inside it. Make sure there are a number of each of the coins previously looked at inside it and also some 10p coins. Show the class an example of each coin and ask them to add up different combinations that you show them. Then draw the money boxes in Figure 1 on the flip chart and ask the children to write down how much money is inside each one.

Ask the children to draw and colour in a number of items they would find in the supermarket, such as apples, bananas or bread. Then get them to cut each picture out and guide them in writing prices next to each of their items. Divide the class into pairs and give each pair a box of coins. One child should show a picture to their partner who has to make up the required amount to pay for it using the coins in the box. Change the pair over so that each child has a chance to use the money. This game can be developed by asking the children to choose the least amount of coins to pay for each item.

Divide the class into pairs again and give each pair a copy of photocopiable page 58 and a box of coins. The coins should be divided between the two children. Taking alternate turns, the children must take only one coin at a time and place it on the goods in the trolley. The aim is to

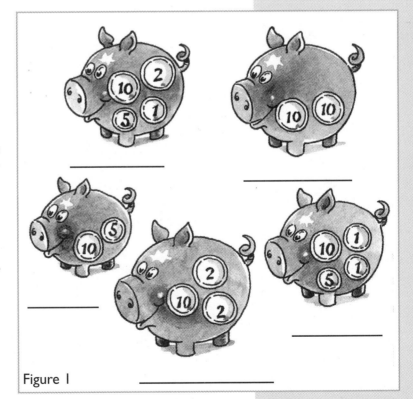

Figure 1

accumulate the correct amount of money on each picture – the first child to do this on all the pictures is the winner. Make sure there are not too many high-value coins in the coin box so that the children have to make up the amounts from different coins. If possible have a checker (this could be a child who has a good knowledge of coin values).

Science

The food that we buy at the market has to be grown and the children should understand the process of growth. Discuss with the class what plants need to grow (light, water, warmth). Explain that they will be trying to grow some cress seeds under different conditions. Talk about what the different conditions might be and guide them in choosing (a dark place, a light place, with water, without water, in the fridge). Divide the class into groups and allocate a different growing environment to each. Get the groups to grow their seeds on absorbent paper (such as a paper towel) placed in a dish. Provide a daily observation chart for the classroom so that the children can keep a record of how the various seeds are growing and discuss the results at the end of the week.

History

Have a discussion with the children about the type of food they eat and the type of food they think that people in Britain used to eat 50–100 years ago. Ask if they think they would have eaten yoghurt, pasta, curry or pizza. Explain that they might have eaten rice pudding, steak and kidney pie, meat with vegetables and steamed puddings. Get the children to prepare a home note asking the older members of their families for information about foods they ate in the past and ask them to return these in the middle of the week.

Refer the children to slips that have been returned and discuss the replies with them, making a list of the foods on the flip chart. Establish why the children eat different food today from that of their parents and grandparents, linking in discussions about travel, efficient transportation and preservation as reasons for the changes in food availability and what people eat.

Ask the children if they know what 'fast food' is and encourage them to talk about whether or not this sort of food is a good idea. Make sure that they consider factors such as cost, nutritional value, convenience and so on. Finish by asking the children to compile two charts of 'Now' and 'Then' food using either information from their own home or from the whole-class discussion earlier.

Geography

Bring the shopping basket of home-grown and foreign-grown foods into the classroom. Show the items to the class and discuss if anyone has seen any of the foods growing – if so, where? Explain where each item comes from and why we can't grow all the food we eat in Britain.

Ask each child to make their own chart like that in Figure 2. Get them to record information about what foods they like to eat that are home-grown inside the circle, and those that are grown abroad outside the circle. Finish by asking volunteers to read out their information to the rest of the class.

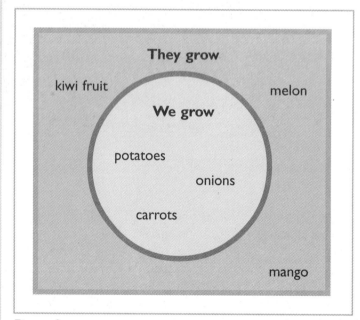

Figure 2

RE

Read with the children 'Tear down this temple' from *The Message* by Eugene Peterson.

TEAR DOWN THIS TEMPLE

When the Passover Feast, celebrated each spring by the Jews, was about to take place, Jesus travelled up to Jerusalem. He found the Temple teeming with people selling cattle and sheep and doves. The money lenders were also there in full strength.

Jesus put together a whip made out of strips of leather and chased them out of the Temple, stampeding the sheep and cattle, upending the tables of the money lenders, spilling coins left and right. He told the dove merchants,

'Get your things out of here! Stop turning my father's house into a shopping centre.'

Point out that this is quite a different Jesus from the quiet and calm man we usually read about. Can the children give any suggestions as to why he was so angry (because the Temple had been made into a market place where people were buying and selling things when it should have been a House of God)? What do the children think about that? Play a circle game, where one child mimes an emotion in the centre of the circle and the others guess which emotion it is. Whoever guesses the emotion takes the mimer's place.

PSHE

Talk to the children about a typical market place. Ask if any of them know how lively the atmosphere can be. Ask the children which things make them feel lively. Which things make them feel calm? Listen to the mood tapes and ask them to describe how they are feeling.

Music

Ask the children to sit in a circle so that you have eye contact with each child. Clap once for the rhythm of the name of a fruit which has a one-beat sound (*peach, pear, plum*), then clap twice for a two-beat fruit (*ap-ple, cher-ry, dam-son*), three times for a three-beat fruit (*rasp-ber-ry, black-cur-rant, straw-ber-ry*) and four times for any four-beat fruit (*pom-e-gran-ate*). Divide the class into four groups and give each the name of a fruit. Clap the names through with the children, then clap yourself a steady four beats, making the first beat louder than the rest. Ask the children to try to fit the sound of their fruit into your beat, always starting a new fruit beat on your first beat, and clap it with you.

Ask the children if any of them have heard the noises in a busy market place. Ask any children who have to talk about the cries the market sellers make to sell their goods, such as *Ripe pears* or *Come and buy my tomatoes*. Ask the children, in pairs, to make up a street cry of their own and to perform it to the rest of the class. Then get all the children to move around the room pretending to sell and sing their cries – noisy, but great fun! Tape the children and play their cries back to them.

Art

Give each child a paper plate and a selection of materials, such as small boxes, straws, shells, pebbles and string. Ask them to create a representation of their favourite foods. When they have finished they can create labels on the computer to attach to each of the foods on their plates.

D&T

Explain to the children that they are going to make a potato bag trolley. Get them to consider different factors before allowing them to design their trolley, such as the size and weight of bags of potatoes and why a trolley might be needed to take potatoes to and from a market. Ask the children to consider what shape would be best for the wheels. Use a selection of different plastic shapes and invite some children to demonstrate why a circle is the best shape for a wheel to be. Then divide the class into groups and ask them to design a trolley using two wheels and an axle. Tell them they should draw a diagram of their design to show how the trolley would be constructed and to include a list of materials needed to make it.

PE

Ask if any of the children have been to Covent Garden in London. Have a few pictures of it to show to the children and explain that it has an area for tumblers, jugglers, puppets, clowns, stilt walkers and acrobats to perform in. Tell the children that they are going to move like these performers in Covent Garden.

   Warm the class up by getting the children to run, jump, hop and skip around the room, and to respond to commands of stop/start. Then ask them to travel on their legs and then crab-like, responding to stop/start commands each time.

   Divide the class into groups of four or five. Place mats in safe, appropriate places around the room and encourage the children to develop different ways of safely travelling across the mat in the style of a tumbler, for example performing forward rolls, backward rolls, sliding, moving on the side of the body and so on.

NOW OR LATER

■ Make a class graph of how tall the cress grows in the science experiment. (mathematics)

■ Design a label for a food packet. Take a variety of colourful packets of food into the classroom for the children to discuss. Look at the lettering and design, talking about what makes them eye-catching. Ask the children to design a label for their favourite food. (D&T)

■ Ask the children to imagine they are having a party and to draw up a shopping list for it. (English)

■ Give the children some thin strips of paper and show them how to weave them together to make the texture of a shopping basket. Then show them how to glue the woven paper on to a drawing of a basket to turn it into a realistic representation. (art)

THE WONDERFUL WIZARD OF OZ

RESOURCES
You will need:
■ photocopiable page 59, flip chart or board, paper, card, writing and colouring materials, access to computers (English)
■ clock face, paper, writing materials, copies of photocopiable page 60 for each child, glue, scissors, coloured paper (mathematics)
■ wires, batteries, bulbs, bulb holders, paper, writing materials (science)
■ paper, writing materials, Blu Tack (geography)
■ flip chart or board, paper, writing materials (PSHE)
■ flip chart or board, selection of musical instruments such as cymbals, xylophones, woodblocks, tape player, tape (music)
■ abstract painting such as a Picasso, paper, paint (art)
■ large pieces of paper or card labelled north, south, east and west (PE).

WHAT TO DO
English
Read to the children the version of *The Wonderful Wizard of Oz* on photocopiable page 59. Ask the children if they can remember the main characters (Dorothy, the Scarecrow, the Lion, the Tin Woodman and the Great Oz). Ask the children if they can think of an adjective to describe each character. Suggest *wonderful* wizard, *gentle* lion and so on. Make a list on the flip chart of the characters and invite the children to write three sentences about each character. Remind the children how to build a sentence using a capital letter at the beginning and a full stop at the end. When they have finished ask them to share their ideas with everyone.

In the story, Dorothy is making her way along the road towards a city of emeralds. Do the children know what colour emeralds are? Ask what other coloured jewels they can think of. Write these down and get the children to think about how many of the colours appear in a rainbow. Read to them the 'Rainbow' poem (see page 42) and use it as a starting point to write a class

OBJECTIVES
■ using adjectives and alliteration; firing the imagination to write a story **(English)**
■ using different activities to reinforce the concept of time **(mathematics)**
■ wiring a circuit **(science)**
■ reinforcing directional language **(geography)**
■ observing courage in other people **(RE)**
■ exploring feelings of bravery and fear **(PSHE)**
■ focusing on the rhythm of words **(music)**
■ appreciating and responding to the work of an artist **(art)**
■ moving in response to instructions **(PE)**

rainbow poem. Collect ideas and words that they suggest on the flip chart and see if they can provide rhyming words to go with them. When the class poem, is complete use it as a handwriting activity by asking each child to copy it out and illustrate it.

RAINBOW

Red is a warm winter hat
Oranges, juicy and fat
Yellow round ball rolling over
Green grass, green clover
Blue skies, the sun peeps through
Indigo, looks a bit blue
Violet, a flower so small
My rainbow poem is for you all.

Build up an atmosphere of anticipation by reminding the children of the road Dorothy was walking along and asking the class to take an imaginary walk along a magic road. Ask them to imagine that there is a signpost by the side of the road. What do the children think it might say? (Suggest *magic land*, *spell shop*, *clouds* to get them started.) Record their ideas and then give them an opening sentence: *I had just walked down the magic road when…* and ask them to write a short story using some of the words from the signpost. Ask some of the children to share their stories with the class.

Ask the children what their wishes would be if they were on the road with Dorothy. How do the children imagine that wizards make wishes come true? Lead the discussion towards spells. Ask the children to suggest things that might be used in a spell and then to use alliteration to describe them, such as *slippery slugs*, *frosty frogs*, *woven webs*, *sparkling stars*. Copy the spell in Figure 3 onto the flip chart and ask each child to complete it in their own way. Get the children to share their spells with each other.

Ask the children what they would include if they were presenting a programme of events on the week's English activities. Remind them of character descriptions, the journey along the road stories, spells and poems about the rainbow. Together decide which would come first and last, and how the other activities would fit in. When it is appropriate ask the children to compile a programme using the computer.

SPELL
In my cauldron
Deep and dark
Throw some things
To make it spark

Figure 3

Mathematics

Tell the children to imagine that they are Dorothy from *The Wonderful Wizard of Oz* story. Ask them what they think she might be doing at certain times of the day. Pick random hours and suggest that at 8 o'clock she might be having breakfast, at 1 o'clock having lunch. Have a clock face to show to the children and ask them to suggest where the fingers should be pointing for each of the times you are talking about. Make sure the children have a lot of practice recognising the hours on the clock.

Check the children's understanding of *am* and *pm*. Show them different times on the clock face and give them an activity that you would be doing at that time, such as going to bed or coming to school. Ask them to provide you with the time shown on the clock, specifying *am* or *pm* each time.

Divide the class into small groups and tell them that they are going to play 'clock lotto'. Explain that you are the caller and will be shouting out different hour times and that in their groups the children should draw clock faces and the position the hands should be in. Call out ten different times and then ask the groups to give you their answers.

Give each child a copy of photocopiable page 60. Tell the children that first they should write the time next to each of the twelve clock faces. Then they will need to

Figure 4

cut out the cards and place them in the order in which a day would progress, stating *am* or *pm* if necessary. Once they have done this, ask them to glue the cards onto a piece of coloured paper in a large circle (see Figure 4).

Science
Explain to the children that they are going to make an electrical circuit that could be used to light up the eyes of a model of the Tin Woodman once he has his brain from the Great Oz.

Divide the class into pairs and give each pair two wires, a battery, a bulb and a bulb holder. Talk to the class about how circuits work by explaining that to make the bulb light up they need to link the battery and the bulb holder, which contains the bulb, to the wires. Give them the freedom to experiment with their apparatus and then ask each pair to comment on their results. Emphasise that the ones that did not work did not have the wires connected firmly. Ask the children to keep a record of the activity by drawing a simple diagram of their circuit.

Geography
Remind the children that in the story of *The Wonderful Wizard of Oz* the writer writes about the Wicked Witch of the East and the Wicked Witch of the West. Do the children know which way is east and which way is west? Invite some of them to show the class which way they think is which. When would the children use the words east and west and where do they think they might see them (for example, weather vanes, sundials, compasses)?

Reinforce the children's understanding of the directions by playing looking games. Tell them to *Look to the east, Turn to the west.*

Ask the children to tell you what they can see in the east of the room and in the west of the room, and make a list of their observations. Be sure that you are facing the same way as the children! Finally, get the children to make some east/west labels for the classroom and allow them to attach them to relevant objects.

RE

Only a boy called David,
only a rippling brook;
only a boy called David,
five little stones he took.
Then one little stone went in the sling,
and the sling went round and round,
one little stone went in the sling,
and the sling went round and round.
Round and round and round and round
round and round and round;
one little stone went up, up, up,
and the giant came tumbling down!

Read this verse about David to the children. It has a catchy tune and can be found in *Junior Praise* (HarperCollins), but also stands well on its own as a poem.

Tell the children the story of David and Goliath (the David Kossoff version in *Bible Stories* published by Fount is excellent or any modern translation). Then refer the children back to the lion in *The Wonderful Wizard of Oz*. Point out that he wanted to be brave, just like David. Can the children retell the story of David in their own words as a writing exercise, remembering how he was brave? This would be an opportune time to dramatise the story in small groups, or to re-sing or say the verse.

PSHE

Ask the children if they can remember that the Lion in *The Wonderful Wizard of Oz* was sad. Can they remember why he felt like that? Remind them that it was because he wanted to be brave and didn't have courage. Lead this into a class discussion about bravery and when the children feel they need to be brave. Collect some words from them that they associate with being brave, (for example, *strong, fearless, courage*).

Ask them what they see as opposite to bravery (*fear, weakness*). Ask what kinds of things they have been frightened of (*the dark, wind, bullies*). Can the children remember situations when they have been frightened and recognise how they have overcome this fear? Give everyone a piece of paper and ask them to write about a situation where they have been brave and a situation where they have felt frightened. Ask if any of the children would like to share their writing with the class and talk about their feelings.

Music

Re-read to the class the spell (Figure 3, page 42), emphasising the rhythm of the words as you read it. Divide the class into small groups and get them to discuss in their groups how best they think they can represent the spell using music. Suggesting a drum beat to copy the word rhythm is a good start. On the flip chart, write the first couple of lines and underline the words where the beat falls to give some guidance. Suggest some other ideas, such as the sound of a cymbal roll on *cauldron*, a low sound on a xylophone for *deep and dark*, jumping sounds on the woodblock for *throw* and an explosion of all the sounds to create a *spark*.

The children will have many ideas to accompany the spell, so give them the opportunity to experiment. If there are only a few instruments available, divide them between the groups and suggest that vocal sounds and body percussion (hand claps or foot stamps) are just as effective. Make time for each group to perform to the class and to comment on each other's interpretations. You could also tape each group's music and play it back to them.

Art

Show the children an abstract painting (any Picasso painting would be a good example) and suggest that this might be what a magic land looked like. Talk with the class about the style of the picture and then give them the opportunity to paint their own magic land in a Picasso style.

PE

Perform warm-up activities with the children by getting them to run and jump, skip and hop around the room.

Label each wall north, south, east and west. Ask the children to stand in the middle of the room and to move to given directions. Call out different directions and instructions about the way the children should move, such as *Jump three paces north*, *Walk south until I say stop*.

Set up a game of 'Islands'. Place four mats underneath the labels on the wall and tell the children to run and land on the island that you call out, such as *Run to the island in the west*. Create some hazards to eliminate children, such as *Those children on the south island are eaten by gorillas*, *Those on the east island are scorched by the Sun*. These children should sit out until a winner is found.

NOW OR LATER

■ Divide the children into small groups and give them an opportunity to create a drama around a spell they have created. (English)

■ Create a class wall-map of the imaginary land that Dorothy visited. It should show her home, the road and the city of emeralds. Everyone should be able to contribute something either artistic or written. (geography)

■ Create stick puppets of the characters in *The Wonderful Wizard of Oz*. Retell the story as the background to a puppet show performed by groups of children. (art)

MESSAGES

OBJECTIVES

■ communicating written and pictorial messages; writing for a purpose and creating mnemonic sentences **(English)**
■ recording number sentences pictorially; using a number line for addition and subtraction and representing mathematical statements horizontally **(mathematics)**
■ exploring properties of materials **(science)**
■ comparing past and present means of written communication **(history)**
■ becoming familiar with and responding to directional language **(geography)**
■ learning the importance of responding to messages **(RE)**
■ converting sound to message **(music)**
■ thinking about other people and responding in a practical and creative way **(art/PSHE)**
■ designing a message system **(D&T)**
■ responding physically to signals **(PE)**

RESOURCES

You will need:
■ *Katie Morag Delivers the Mail* by Mairi Hedderwick (Red Fox), flip chart or board, paper, writing materials, cave painting picture, white chalk, black sugar paper, copies of photocopiable page 61 for each child (English)
■ a selection of objects such as envelopes, pencils, stamps or parcels, flip chart, paper, pens and pencils, number lines from 1–15, digit cards, dice (mathematics)
■ materials for making a seal such as sand, clay, mud, wax, plaster of Paris, Plasticine, cotton wool; paper, pencils (science)
■ a selection of old and new writing instruments such as a quill, a pen with a nib, ink, fountain pen, biro; flip chart or board, access to computers (history)
■ chalk, copies of photocopiable page 62 for each child (geography)
■ paper, writing materials (RE)
■ large sheet of card, paper, pens and pencils, tambourines, drums, triangles or other percussion instruments (music)
■ A4 card, potato halves, apple, pear or tomato halves, corks, shells, wheels, paint (art)
■ coloured tissue paper, marker pens, 'Get Well' cards started in art (PSHE)
■ cardboard boxes, tins, rubber bands, crunchy paper, plastic pots, paper, writing materials (D&T)
■ whistle, benches, mats, coloured bands, batons (PE).

WHAT TO DO

English

Read aloud to the class *Katie Morag Delivers the Mail* by Mairi Hedderwick. Ask the children to think of nouns that would relate to a postman delivering the mail (*mail, messages, parcel, letter, birthday card*) and write the words on the flip chart. Talk about messages with the children and encourage them to suggest what could be in a message they might receive (*Please come to my party* or *Happy Birthday to you*). Ask the children to write their own messages and to read some of their messages to each other.

Introduce the children to writing for a purpose by talking to them about the idea of running a book sale in aid of Comic Relief. Ask them how they think they could advertise it and where. Tell the children that they are going to write an advertisement for the book sale to be placed in the local newspaper. Ask them to suggest what information they think they should include and write their ideas on the flip chart. Make sure that the children include time, date, place, book sale and Comic Relief in the list. Ask the children to write the advertisement containing all the information and then ask some of them to read their work aloud.

Explain to the children that one of the earliest ways of remembering things was to make a mnemonic sentence with initial letters. Explain what this means

and give examples, such as *Richard Of York Gave Battle In Vain* for the rainbow, or *Never Eat Shredded Wheat* for compass directions. Ask the children to create a mnemonic sentence for the seasons (*SSAW*), the traffic light sequence (*RAG*), the suits in a pack of cards (*HCDS*) or for road safety (*Right Left Right Again*). Get them to share their ideas with the class.

Show the children the picture of a cave wall painting and explain how cave people used to leave messages in their caves this way. What do the children think the message in the picture shows? Remind them of the story *Katie Morag Delivers the Mail* and ask if Katie were to leave a message like this on the island where do the children think she would have drawn it – on the sand or the rocks? What do they think she would use to draw with? Give each child some white chalk and black sugar paper and ask them to draw a message. On another piece of paper invite them to record the same message in words. Look together at the different ways of conveying the messages. Talk with the children about which way of conveying the messages is clearer.

Give each child a copy of photocopiable page 61 and tell them they are going to look for writing words. Show the children how to use a wordsearch, explaining how they should look for and record the words. The children could work with a partner to complete the wordsearch if they find it difficult. More able children could compose a wordsearch for other class members to complete.

Mathematics

First of all introduce the children to the idea of recording number sentences using pictures. Show the children a selection of easy-to-draw objects (envelopes, pencils, stamps or parcels). Bring the children together into a large circle and in the centre place different combinations of these objects. Encourage the children to count, add and subtract them. Write the example in Figure 5 on a flip chart and ask the children to record their own number sentences using pictures of what they counted in the circle.

Tell the children that a long time ago, before people were familiar with numbers, tradespeople left messages to show how many bags of corn had been sold to a house by placing a peg into a hole in

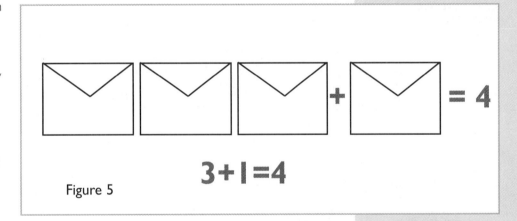

3+1=4

Figure 5

the wall. Another way of leaving a number message was to make a notch in a stick. Explain that from this the idea of the number line was developed. Some children will already be familiar with number lines but it is always useful to remind them of the procedure for addition and subtraction. To begin with draw a large number line on the flip chart to work with the whole class, asking them to volunteer answers to your addition and subtraction questions. Then give each child a number line from 1–15 and allow the children individual experience in using a number line to add or subtract. The number line can be extended for children capable of working with larger numbers.

Show the children some digit cards and explain that they will be using these to generate numbers for horizontal addition. Show the children how by placing the digit cards horizontally they are creating a line of random numbers, for example 9, 7, 3, 4. Explain that by putting an addition sign between them they become a number sentence. Can they quickly add the numbers together?

Ask the children to work in pairs. Give each pair a set of digit cards and place them face down on the desk. Tell the pairs to number themselves 1 and 2, and then ask all the number 1's to turn over a card. Both children in the pair should record the number. Then tell all the number 2's to do the same. When the children have four numbers recorded they should write an addition sign between each to make a number sentence and add up the total. Continue with this activity, asking them to subtract the totals on alternate rounds.

Invite two children to demonstrate to the class how to play the game 'Nearest to 20'. Ask them to take turns throwing a dice and record their respective numbers in two large circles on a flip chart. After they have each thrown five times ask them to add their numbers together. Then ask the class who achieved the score nearest to 20. Ask the children to play the game with a partner, recording their own results.

Science
Explain to the children how important letters used to be sent in the past with a special seal on the back of the envelope so that the sender could be clearly identified. Explain that these seals had the sender's initials or coat of arms on them. Tell the children they are going to make a seal that includes their own initials. Show them a variety of materials that they could use (see Resources) and ask them to predict which will be the most effective. Give them enough time to try out the different materials in groups, explaining that they should look out for materials which can be moulded or marked in a permanent way. Get the children to come together as a class to discuss each group's results and when they have established which material is best give each child an opportunity to make their own individual seal and to use it.

History
Discuss with the children ways in which people communicated in the past (drums, smoke signals, cave paintings and so on). Then show the children the selection of old and modern writing instruments (see Resources) to show the development of

communication by words and writing. Talk about each of the writing instruments with the class and ask the children who they think might have used them. Encourage the children to think about the sort of people who would have done a lot of writing in the past (a scribe, a clerk, a doctor) and who would use the modern writing instruments today (everyone). Record their suggestions on the flip chart and ask the children to consider why more people write today (for example, better education and technology).

Set up a writing table so that the children can experiment with the different writing tools.

Discuss the different ways people write today and lead the class towards thinking about the importance of word-processing. During the week provide an opportunity for each child to write a birthday message using a word-processing programme on the computer for anyone they wish. Encourage them to use an animated software programme to make their message more exciting.

Geography
Draw a large representation of the compass points on the floor or playground. Talk with the children about the position of north, south, east and west – can any of them show the rest of the class which way they point? Then allow the children to familiarise themselves with the directions by calling out instructions such as *walk two*

steps north, *three steps east*, *three steps south* and *four steps west*, and so on. Continue to let them practise in this way until most of the children are confident with the directions.

Arrange a treasure hunt to find a message hidden in the classroom or playground. Give oral instructions to the children using directional language, *right, left, forwards, backwards, under, over, north, south, east* and *west* to reinforce the meaning of the terms.

Give the children a copy of photocopiable page 62. Ask them to record the four routes to take the post bag to the road where the post van can pick it up, using compass points and number of squares travelled as their descriptions (route A has been done for them).

RE

Explain to the children how in some faiths the rules of the religion were sent to people through messages.

Muslims have five main duties to perform, which they believe were given to them in a message from God and were told to them by the Prophet Muhammad. These rules of how to live are to be found in the Koran, a Holy book. They believe that there is only one true God, Allah, and that Muhammad is his messenger. Muslims must pray five times a day, give money to good causes, not eat or drink between dawn and dusk during one month of the year (Ramadan) and they should visit Mecca once in their lifetime. Muslims have many other rules to live by to become good Muslims, such as not eating pork, their meat should be prepared in a special way (Halal), not drinking alcohol, not gambling or fighting, not be mean and be kind to strangers.

Jews and Christians both believe that Moses, a prophet, gave them a message from God that told them how they should live. This message was written on a tablet of stone at Mount Sinai and is called the Ten Commandments. The Jews read these in the Talmut and the Christians can find it in the Old Testament of the Bible. These rules say:

■ worship only God
■ don't make any idols or statues and worship them
■ don't speak God's name in a false way
■ keep Sunday special for worshipping God
■ be respectful of your father and mother
■ don't kill
■ be faithful to your husband or wife
■ don't steal
■ don't tell lies
■ don't be envious of the things other people have.

Talk to the children about the Muslim rules and compare them with the Jewish and Christian rules. Ask them to point out the similarities and differences. Emphasise the importance of rules so that people can live together in harmony. Explain to the children that sometimes unhappy things occur in the outside world, such as war, disease, murder, famine, quarrels and fighting, because people don't observe the 'living together' rules. Go on to explain that sometimes unhappy things happen in the classroom too. Help the children to create a scroll of rules for the week and put them up in the classroom. Set up a reward system for children who comply with these rules.

Music
Ask the children to sit in a big circle. In the middle of the circle place a large sheet of card and writing materials. Then give some of the children the percussion instruments and ask them one at a time to play a variety of sounds, such as shaking a tambourine, banging a drum, sounding one triangle note. Invite different children to write on the large sheet of card in picture language how they would represent the sound (you may want to draw the first example such as one of those in Figure 6). Tell the children that this is graphic notation and is an easy way to remember and pass on information about sounds to others. Encourage the children to write by prompting them to describe short sounds, long sounds, high and low sounds, loud and soft sounds.

Divide the children into pairs. Each pair will need a long piece of paper, a pencil and a few instruments. Ask them to create a short piece of music using a range of different sounds and to record it using graphic notation. Then ask them to give their recorded sounds to another pair and see if they can play each other's compositions.

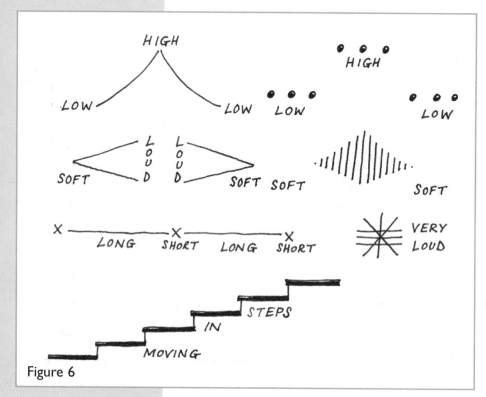
Figure 6

Art
Tell the children they are going to make a 'Get Well' card. Give each child a piece of A4 card and get them to fold it in half. Show them how to create repeating patterns to form a background, using the apples, pears or tomatoes which have been cut in half, or shaped potatoes dipped in paint for printing. Other suitable materials, such as corks, wheels or shells could be used as an alternative.

PSHE
Ask the children if they have ever visited someone in hospital or someone who is ill. Encourage any of those who have to talk about this to the class. Ask the children to make suggestions as to how ill people can be cheered up.

Suggest that a 'Get Well' card can be a good way and continue making the one started in art. Provide the coloured tissue paper for the children to make 3-D flowers for the front of the card and to write Get well soon or another message on the front. If any of the children know someone who is ill they could address a message inside the card to that person.

D&T
Talk to the children about different ways of sending messages. Direct the children's thoughts to sound messages and suggest a simple way of creating sound is to make a sound box. Ask them what they think might be needed to make a sound box. Point out that they will need to make a hole in the box and something to make sound with. Draw an example on the flip chart of how it could look (see Figure 7).

Ask the children to design their own sound box and provide materials (see Resources) from which they can choose what to make it with. Show them how

50

Ready to go! SUPPLY TEACHING

Figure 7

laying rubber bands tightly over an opening in a box or tin allows the bands to be strummed like a guitar to create a sound. Allow the children to make the box that they have designed, decorate it and try out its sound. Design a code with the class and ask some children to send and other children to interpret the messages.

PE
Warm the children up by asking them to run around without touching each other. Tell them that you will send messages telling them to change direction and that the signal will be a whistle blow. Next ask them to focus on jumping and landing with their feet together and then apart. Remind the children that they should land softly. Using benches and mats, ask them to carry out activities such as walking along the bench forwards and backwards, hopping around the mat and jumping off the bench onto the mats.

Divide the class into teams of four – red, yellow, green and blue. Give each team appropriate colour bands and ask them to number themselves 1–4. Then tell the children to sit in a large circle in team order. At a given signal all the number 1's, carrying a baton or an object, run to the right around the circle and back to their place giving the baton to number 2. Number 2 hops round the circle, returning to give the baton to number 3. Continue in this way until all the children have had a turn. The first team to finish and sit down is the winner. Suggest to the children that in the same teams they devise an alternative game of their own.

NOW OR LATER
■ Encourage the idea of letter writing with a purpose. Suggest the children write a 'Thank you' message. (English)
■ Create a coded message by using a series of rhythmical hand claps to represent letters. One child should clap the message while the class tries to recognise it. (music)
■ Develop the idea of using graphic notation as a musical message system. Divide the class into groups and get each group to create their own scores. The groups could then exchange their scores and play each other's music to the rest of the class. (music)

WHITE

OBJECTIVES

■ writing in a formal style; using adjectives; researching information and compiling a factual piece of writing **(English)**
■ recognising and drawing symmetrical images, and understanding basic fractions **(mathematics)**
■ discovering the changing states of materials **(science)**
■ carrying out geographical enquiries **(geography)**
■ respecting customs in different cultures **(RE)**
■ considering other people's feelings **(PSHE)**
■ creating sound effects to represent poetic meaning **(music)**
■ expressing ideas using collage materials **(art)**
■ experimenting with flavours **(D&T)**
■ using the body to represent a natural object **(PE)**

RESOURCES

You will need:

■ white items such as a feather, a handkerchief or a plate; flip chart or board, table, digital camera, paper, writing and colouring materials, reference books or CD-ROMs on animals (English)
■ black and white paper, white paint, A4 white paper, scissors, glue, coloured paper, writing materials, flip chart, white board(s), 10cm pieces of string, items to cut into pieces such as bread or cakes, copies of photocopiable page 63 for each child, counters marked ½ and ¼ on either side (mathematics)
■ ice cubes, balloons filled with water and frozen (science)
■ snowscape pictures (these are easily obtained from pictures of winter months on calendars, travel brochures, postcards or books), paper, writing materials (geography)
■ white sheet or tablecloth, colourful cloth, recorders, drums (RE)
■ soft-sounding percussion instruments such as triangles, glockenspiels, chime bars, bells, tambourines, cabasa, vibraslap, agogo bells (music)
■ a copy of *The Lion, the Witch and the Wardrobe* by CS Lewis, black sugar paper, white materials such as polystyrene, fabric, sequins, metallic paper, tinsel, cardboard; glue (art)
■ milk shake ingredients: strawberry syrup, chocolate syrup (pre-made with caster sugar, water and cocoa powder, see activity), milk, vanilla ice cream, bowl or jug, whisk, plastic beakers (D&T).

WHAT TO DO

English

Take into the classroom a selection of things that are white, for example paper, a feather, a handkerchief, a plate. Ask the children to describe the items and discover what they all have in common. Tell the children that they have all had an imaginary invitation to a 'white party', where white is the theme. Encourage discussion amongst the children about what characters they would like to go as, for example a ghost, a polar bear, a snowman, a snowflake, a feather and so on. Choose a few of the best suggestions and ask the children to describe these costumes, making a list of words they use on the flip chart, such as *shiny, sparkling, dazzling, glowing, bright, glittery*.

Invite the children to reply to the imaginary invitation. Write out the example in Figure 8 for the class to see. Ask them to fill in the acceptance using some of the adjectives listed on the flip chart to describe how they will be dressed.

WHITE PARTY ACCEPTANCE

——————— will be delighted to attend

the White Party on ——————— at ———————————————

at ——————— pm. He/she will be coming as a ———————————

The costume will be ———————————————————————

Figure 8

Invite some children to read their descriptions of their 'white party' character and to mime actions relating to their choice of character. Explain that the party is going to take place, but no one will be speaking. Ask the class what actions their characters might use. Encourage the use of –ing words, such as *waving, walking, eating, chatting, dancing* and make a list of them. Ask the children, in the role of their character, to respond in mime to each of the words as you read them out. Then place a table in the centre of the room and invite each character on a signal to approach the table and freeze in a party position. If a digital camera is available, take photographs of the finished tableaux.

Read the 'Snow' poem to the children.

SNOW
It fell quietly, like a blanket in the night
Covering the ground, what a lovely sight
Building snowmen
Throwing snowballs
Soft as cotton wool
White as white
Children laughing, shouting, fun
Sledging down the hill they come
Fingers nipping in the cold
Toes wet… so… Here we go!

Then ask them to suggest snow words, for example *cold, crisp, icy, snowball, sledge*, and record them on the flip chart. Ask the children to suggest words that rhyme with some of them, such as *cold/bold, sledge/ledge, bite/light, crunchy/munchy*. Write a collaborative poem with the whole class. Ask the children to copy the poem in their best handwriting, illustrate it and try to write a second verse on their own. Invite some of the children to read their verses to the class.

Ask the children to imagine that they are in a hot-air balloon, travelling slowly over a snow-covered land. Ask if they would like to do this in reality, where they might be going and what they might see. Suggest that the land looks magical under a blanket of snow and compile a list of magical adjectives with the children, such as *surprising, glittering, glowing, sparkling, eerie*. Use the opening sentence *It was a night of magic and I opened my eyes to see everything around me dancing and flying away. I felt my feet…* and ask the children to write a story about what happens next. Ask some of the children to share their stories.

Read to the children the information on the arctic hare.

THE ARCTIC HARE
During the summer the arctic hare has a brown fur coat. As the winter approaches and the days become shorter and the nights longer, white hairs appear in the brown fur. Gradually the whole fur coat becomes white. The arctic hare's colour hides it from its enemies. In winter when the ground is covered in snow the arctic hare can hardly be seen. In the summer when it changes back into brown it is camouflaged against the bare rocks.

Invite them to tell you any facts that they remember from the first reading. Ask if any of the children have seen white hares in Scotland. Can they think of any other white animals (polar bear, white dog, white cat, rabbit, horse, arctic fox)? Tell them to each choose a white animal and allow each child an opportunity to look in a classroom reference book or use a CD-ROM to find any information about their chosen animal. Get them to write their own short piece of information, illustrate it and make it ready for an 'Animal information' book to be compiled with all the children's white animal writing in.

Mathematics

Discuss with the children how the shape of a snowflake is symmetrical. Create a symmetrical pattern to reinforce the children's understanding of symmetry. Paint a quick pattern in white paint onto black paper, fold the paper, smooth it over and open it out. Show the children the results and ask them to comment on what they see. Try several more. The shapes will be different but the symmetry should be obvious.

Give each child a sheet of white paper. Ask them to fold it in half and draw half an image, such as half a snowman, half a white flower or half a candle, against the fold. They should then cut round the image keeping the paper folded and open the paper up. Ask them to comment on what has happened (they should have a whole image). The shapes can be glued onto paper and the line of symmetry indicated. The children should write a statement, for example: *Each of the shapes look the same on either side of the line of symmetry.*

Underline the concept of symmetry by sharing with the class some of the children's examples. On a white board draw half of several images and then ask children to come and draw the other half. If individual white boards are available allow the children to practise drawing symmetrical drawings in this way, or draw a series of half images for the children to copy and complete on their own. Discuss some of them with the class.

Introduce the children to fractions by giving them a piece of string (about 10cm long). Ask them to cut it in half. Discuss what they have done by talking about half of the string and showing them that both pieces make up the whole. Now ask them to cut each piece in half again and talk in the same way about quarters. Get the children to stick the string onto a piece of paper and label the fractions. Next give them a rectangular and a square piece of paper. On the first one ask the children to colour in one half and on the other ask them to colour a quarter. Discuss these fractions with the children and get them to glue their work on to paper and label the fractions as before.

Continue to reinforce the concept of fractions by taking into the classroom suitable items to divide up (a block of vanilla ice cream or a regular slice of bread) which you can show the children how to cut in half and then into quarters. It would be fun to have individual cakes for small groups to cut up and identify a half and a quarter.

Next introduce the fraction game. Divide the class into pairs and give each pair the counter with a half indicated on one side and a quarter on the other. Give each child a copy of photocopiable page 63. Tell them to take turns flipping the counter. They should colour the appropriate fraction on one of the drawings on their sheet according to which side is showing and write the fraction next to the shape.

Science

Talk to the children about snow and ice and what happens when they are brought into the classroom. Discuss with them the process of thawing. Through questions and answers establish the concept that when you make a snowball or hold an ice cube your fingers feel very cold – the snow or ice seems to creep into your fingers. However, explain that what is really happening is that the heat from your fingers is going into the snowball or the ice cube. It melts some of the snow or ice and turns it into water. Have some ice cubes to demonstrate this process.

Talk with the children about how they think snow and ice are formed. Show them some balloons that have been filled with water and frozen. Ask the children to feel them as they begin to thaw and invite them to comment on their observations. Allow the children to record the process in sequenced pictures and to write statements about the stages of thawing.

Geography

For this geographical enquiry the children will need to see pictures of snowscapes, (see Resources). Choose a large picture, easily visible to all the children, and ask a series of questions about it, such as *Can you describe it? Where do you think it is?*

Divide the class into groups of three. Give each group a winter picture and ask them to write a series of observations about what they see. Ask them to address the questions discussed previously, and also what they think it would look like in the summer and why.

RE

Ask the children how many of them have been to a wedding recently. Has anyone been a bridesmaid or a pageboy? Ask any children that respond what faith the married couple belonged to. Explain that in the Christian church it has been traditional for the bride to wear white, but that this is changing. Can the children describe a white wedding dress they have seen recently? This could have been in a shop or a book. Explain that in the Muslim religion, the bride wears very bright colours and much jewellery. Ask the children to describe and talk about any Muslim brides they have seen.

Do the children know of any other differences? Tell them that a traditional Christian wedding usually takes place in a church and a priest, vicar or minister takes the service. The bride is given away to her fiancé by her father. They usually have a party afterwards and go away together on a honeymoon. At a Muslim wedding the couple have to ask to be married in front of The Qadi (a judge) and he sets the dowry (an amount of money) to be paid by the bridegroom to the bride. The marriage is blessed by a reading from the Koran (the Holy Book) and sweets are then given to the guests. The next day the Walima (party) is held and the bridegroom wears a special head-dress.

Divide the class into groups telling them they are going to act out the stages of the two different weddings. Give one group a white sheet or tablecloth and the other a colourful cloth to represent the dresses of the brides. Ask each group to allocate roles (bride, groom and guests) and perform to each other. Some of the children in each group could provide music, using recorders to create suitable hymn music for the Christian wedding, and drums and voices for the Muslim wedding.

PSHE

Ask the children if they know what a 'white lie' is. Give an example where the statement would be, *She doesn't like your dog* and the white lie would be *She didn't say that she didn't like your dog, she said she doesn't like dogs.* Explain that a white lie is a lie that hides the truth so as not to hurt someone's feelings. Can the children think of any examples of white lies they might tell to avoid upsetting someone?

Music

Read the poem 'Snow' (see page 53) to the class. Ask the children if they think they should make loud or soft sounds to describe it using instruments. Divide the children into small groups and allocate the percussion instruments to them (see Resources). Read the poem again while each group takes it in turns making appropriate musical sound effects, for example *sledging down* could be a high to a low sound, *blanket* could be a long continuous sound. Invite the children to comment on each other's sound effects.

Art

Read to the children the description of the Snow Queen from *The Lion the Witch and the Wardrobe* by CS Lewis. Invite the children to describe their ideas of a Snow Queen. Discuss how the children could make a collage picture of a Snow Queen on black sugar paper and then give the children a selection of the white materials you have collected and ask them to represent their Snow Queen. Display the children's work.

D&T

Do the children know that at one time milk was provided in small bottles for every child in the school? Ask them if they know why we drink milk (healthy bones and teeth). Do the children like milk? Ask how they most enjoy their milk (cold, hot, milk shake). Tell the children that they are going to make a milk shake together. Ask the children what they think they will need to make a milk shake and write a list on the flip chart (make sure they include equipment and ingredients). Follow the recipe below.

RECIPE FOR CHOCOLATE MILK SHAKE

Each child will need:
1 tablespoon chocolate syrup
125ml chilled milk
1 scoop of vanilla ice cream

Prepare the chocolate syrup in advance. To make 250ml chocolate syrup mix together six tablespoons of castor sugar with 125ml water and 4 tablespoons of cocoa powder. Bring to the boil, simmer for 1 minute, then whisk until smooth. Allow to cool.

For strawberry milk shake, follow the above instructions for chocolate milk shake substituting strawberry syrup for the chocolate syrup.

PE

Tell the children that they are going to be moving around like snowflakes. Warm the children up by asking them to run, stand still and then run again in different directions, taking care to avoid bumping into each other.

For the main activity encourage the children to use each part of their bodies – hands, feet, head, arms, legs – to stretch and retract whilst standing. Extend this idea by instructing them to perform quick, spiky movements and then contrast these with slow, curved movements. Tell the children to shake their bodies and try again. Then ask them to repeat the activity sitting and then lying down.

In pairs ask the children to mirror each other stretching and curling, changing the leader over frequently. Choose some good examples to demonstrate to the other children. Develop this into an activity for groups of four children. Tell each group to work in a circle making curved shapes inwards and sharp shapes outwards. Encourage a variety of movements.

NOW OR LATER

■ Use Vivaldi's 'Winter' from *The Four Seasons* for the children to perform a creative piece of movement to. (PE)
■ Get the children to create a 3-D snowman using modelling clay and other free-standing material. (art)
■ Show the children a picture of a Tudor house and ask if they know why many of them were black and white. Compare Tudor houses with the children's own homes. (history)

Name

Date

My favourite things

Fruit 	Vegetables 	Drinks 	Dairy produce 

A B C D E F G H I J K L M N O P Q R S T U V W X Y Z

Write your favourite things. Can you put them in alphabetical order?

Ready to go! SUPPLY TEACHING

Shopping trolley

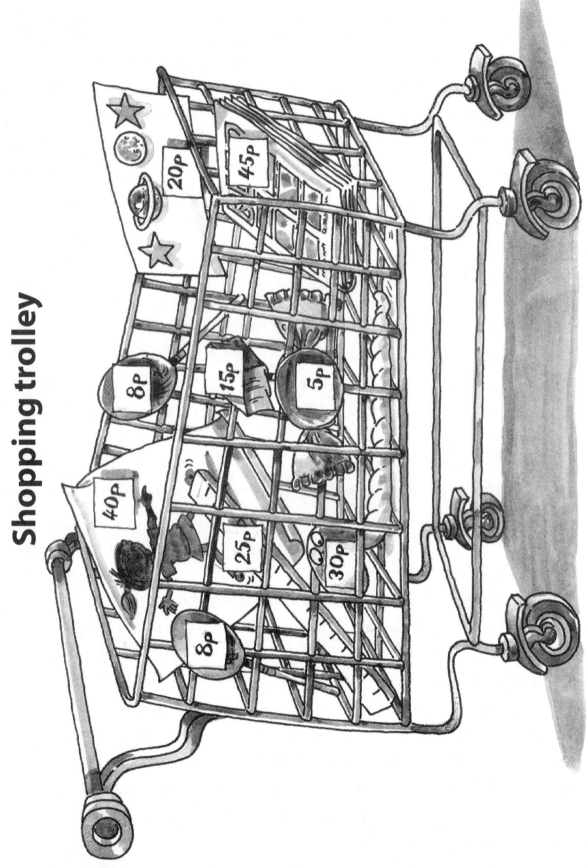

Cover the goods with coins.

📖 SCHOLASTIC

Ready to go! SUPPLY TEACHING

The Wonderful Wizard of Oz

Once upon a time there was a little girl called Dorothy. One day she was sitting in her garden, daydreaming, when all of a sudden she noticed in front of her a long and winding road. It hadn't been there before she thought, so she got up to investigate. The road looked very inviting and since she had nothing better to do, she decided to step onto it and to walk a little way. In the distance she could see the most beautiful City of Emeralds. "Oh I wish I could reach it," she said to herself, and quickened her step.

Suddenly a Lion bounded out onto the road, but instead of roaring at Dorothy, he looked at her sadly. "What's the matter?" said Dorothy.

"I'm so sad," he said. "I'm not very brave and all the other lions laugh at me."

"Why are you here?" asked Dorothy.

"I've been told that if I find the Great Wizard of Oz, who lives in the City of Emeralds, he will make me brave," said the Lion, "but I don't know which way to go because it's through the land of the West Witch."

"Come with me," said Dorothy. "I've come from the East so if we carry along this road we must be heading to the West and we'll reach the Great Oz together."

The Lion cheered up considerably, held her hand and together they walked towards the City of Emeralds. Just then they saw a Tin Woodman, moving slowly and very awkwardly, in front of them. He too looked very sad. Dorothy asked him what was the matter.

"I'm sad because I have no heart," he said, "and I'd love to have a heart. I've been told to find the Great Oz and he will help."

"We're going to see him," said Dorothy. "Come along with us."

Dorothy took his hand, told him about the Lion and together they walked towards the West. A little further along the road they came across a Scarecrow who was placed high on a pole in a cornfield.

"Oh dear, oh dear," Dorothy heard him sigh. "How ever will I find him?"

"Are you looking for the Great Oz?" said Dorothy, "because we're going there too."

"I am indeed," said the Scarecrow. "Can I come too? You see I'm all stuffed with straw and I haven't got a brain and I think he might give me one."

"I'm sure if there are four of us the Wizard will be kind to us," said Dorothy, "and maybe, just maybe, will be able to help."

So they lifted the Scarecrow from the pole and off they went.

Clock loop

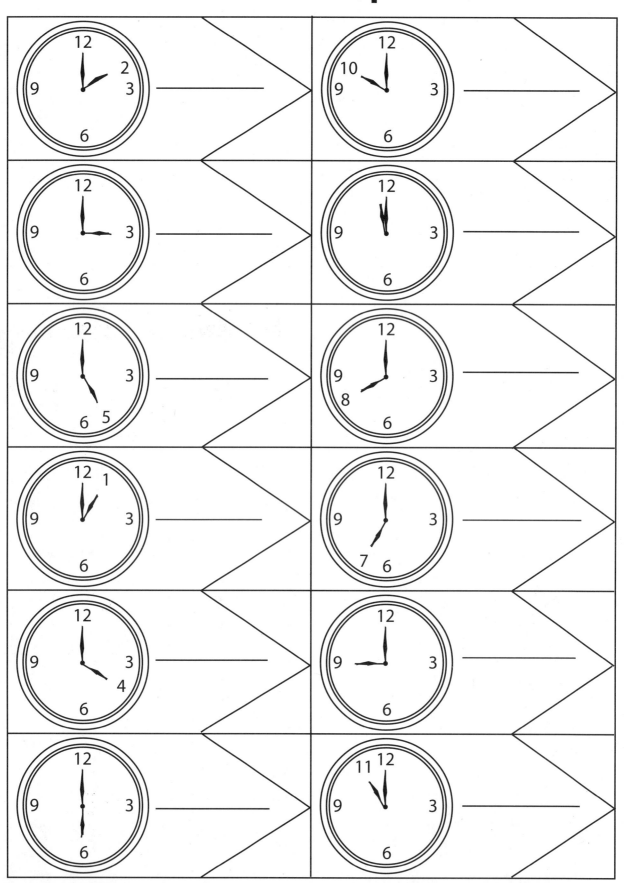

Ready to go! SUPPLY TEACHING